PACKAGING YOUR CRAFTS

A RotoVision book

Published and distributed
by RotoVision SA
Route Suisse 9
CH-1295 Mies
Switzerland

RotoVision SA
Sales and Editorial Office
Sheridan House, 114 Western Road
Hove BN3 1DD, UK

Tel: +44 (0)1273 72 72 68
Fax: +44 (0)1273 72 72 69
www.rotovision.com

10 9 8 7 6 5 4 3 2 1

ISBN: 978-2-88893-223-9

Commissioning Editor: Isheeta Mustafi
Assistant Editor: Tamsin Richardson
Art Director: Lucy Smith
Design Concept: Emily Portnoi
Layout: Suzy McGrath & Lucy Smith
Cover Design: Lucy Smith
Picture Research: Heidi Adnum
Tutorial Photography: Elephant Ideas and Design

Printed in China

ACKNOWLEDGMENTS

My gratitude goes out to the many wonderful
designers, makers, and photographers for their
submission of content and images for the book.
Phillip Ting of Elephant Ideas and Design was
instrumental in photographing all of the tutorials.
The entire project would not have been possible
without the RotoVision team, with special thanks
to Isheeta Mustafi for fearlessly steering the book
to completion, and editor Claire Spinks who tirelessly
spent many a night burning the midnight oil with me.

My heartfelt thanks to Mom and Dad for always
believing in me. Most of all, I thank my husband,
Phillip—packaging extraordinaire and my daily dose
of inspiration, plus Maika, my daughter, who reminds
me every day of the beauty of making. This book is
for you.

Image Credits

Front cover (from left to right): Letterpress printed
tags and printed wraps by Alischa Herrmann, Bespoke
Letterpress; Repurposed egg carton with adhesive label
by Dominique Gros, L'art de la Curiosité; Felt DVD sleeve by
Nikki Mihalik, Akula Kreative.
Back cover (from left to right): Coasters wrapped with
letterpress printed bellybands by Alischa Herrmann,
Bespoke Letterpress; Tea towel with pre-printed, recycled
tag and bound with braid by Leonie Cheung, Papercookie.

PACKAGING YOUR CRAFTS

Creative ideas for crafters, artists, bakers, and more

Viola E. Sutanto

RotoVision

CONTENTS

Section one

MATERIALS AND HOW TO USE THEM

Section two
DESIGNING YOUR PACKAGING

Section three
RESOURCES

Opposite: Hand-decorated, glassine-lined bags by Danie Pout, BLANK.
This page: Digitally cut flowers with paper-wrapped box, by Anastasia Mikailenko, Anastasia Marie.

INTRODUCTION

As a little girl, I always loved wrapping gifts. Whether it was selecting gift wrapping or doodling on brown paper, I was constantly experimenting with different materials and techniques, playing with folds and pleats, ribbons, rubber stamps, you name it. As a finishing touch, I would draw little cards or attach tags. Little did I know, those early days of crafting were the beginning of my love affair with handmade packaging.

Fast forward a couple of decades, I had fully immersed myself in the world of graphic design, creating brand packaging for clients' products. While beautiful and perfectly printed, I missed the tactile experience of using my hands to embellish a package. I was also very interested in the use of recycled and sustainably produced materials. This led me to develop a collection of reusable fabric wraps that eventually became a part of my product line.

With the steady growth of the DIY (do-it-yourself) and the crafter-maker movement, it seems obvious that thoughtful packaging would play a key role in the sales process. Many sellers on Etsy, Folksy, and other craft sites now market their products as "ready to gift." I truly believe that handmade packaging does not have to be complicated or "perfect." In fact, it should be fun! There is often beauty in the unexpected splotch or crease. They help remind the recipient that the object was packaged with love, by hand.

ABOUT THIS BOOK

The first section covers packaging materials such as paper, plastic, fabric, and recycled matter, plus creative ways of using those materials. I have also included some simple, yet effective tutorials to help you get started creating your signature packaging. Each tutorial also features a fictional company and demonstrates a handmade technique that solves a packaging challenge for its brand.

The second section covers a wide range of products and inspired ways of packaging them, along with designer interviews full of practical information to guide your packaging decisions.

You can make wonderful packaging for everything. You'll see how easy it is to build boxes for your needle arts, dress up mason jars containing your specialty preserves, protect one of your delectable cupcakes from being jostled and bashed up after purchase, or create unique hangtags with your brand identity—

in fact, the possibilities are endless! All you need are a few inexpensive supplies (things you may already have if you're a crafter), and some inspiration—which this book aims to provide! Once your creative juices are flowing, you'll no doubt come up with your own take on some of the ideas presented here.

Please don't feel like you have to sit down and read this book from cover to cover; it has been designed for you to dip in and out of as you wish. My hope is that this book will serve both as a useful resource and also as guidance and encouragement, whether you're a veteran seller or an unseasoned newbie!

Opposite: Food box decorated with scrap paper and washi tape by Beatriz Gaspar, Con Botas De Agua.
This page: Patterned kraft paper bag tied with twine by Leonie Cheung, Papercookie.

BRANDING BASICS

There's been a lot of buzz in craft circles around the term "branding" lately, especially among startups and entrepreneurs, and certainly, there is no shortage of definitions for the term. But here is one of my favorites from brand guru Walter Landor: *"Simply put, a brand is a promise. By identifying and authenticating a product or service, it delivers a pledge of satisfaction and quality."*

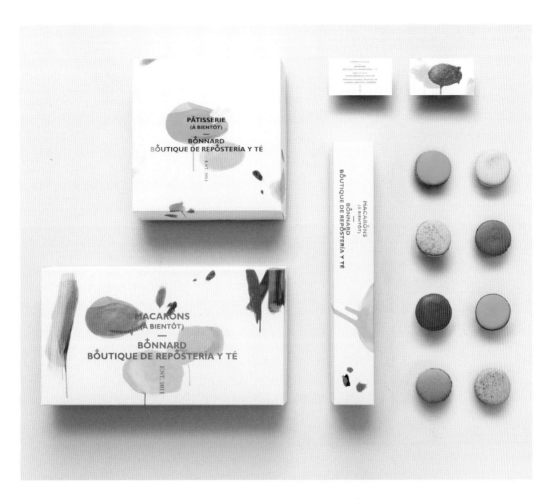

In other words, your brand is more than just your company name, your logo, or even your product. Your brand is the culmination of the experience a customer has with your company from the moment they are introduced to it. It includes your product, its packaging, your website, your company's marketing collateral and advertising campaigns, customer service, and any other aspect of the business that customers may come into contact with.

Every brand has a story to tell, and your packaging is a way of doing that. Think about the message you want to convey to your customer. Does your brand stand for superior construction? Is it an eco-friendly brand? Is extraordinary freshness a key element in your product? Are you a jewelry maker who creates

hip and edgy accessories? Or a hat maker with a passion for vintage designs? How do your current customers perceive your brand? What are the strengths you want to play up? These are all good questions to ask, and from your answers, make a list of adjectives or brand attributes that will help you understand who you are and what your brand is, and will guide you in your packaging decisions.

Opposite: Paper wrapping and stickers by Beatrice Menis.
This page: Gold foil-stamped printed boxes by Bonnard; design by Anagrama.

STORYTELLING THROUGH PACKAGING

The presentation of your product is an important aspect of communicating your brand. Let's break down the information that needs to be present in the packaged product:

- company name and logo
- description of the product (e.g., a candle)
- marketing message (e.g. ,a hand-poured candle made of 100 percent beeswax)
- flavors and ingredients; product style, color, and size (e.g., mandarin orange and rosemary; maxi dress, black, medium)
- images or graphic elements that help identify and differentiate the brand
- instructions for use
- endorsements (e.g., fair-trade, recommendations from the media)
- website and contact information
- any other information required by regulations (e.g., ingredients, warnings, expiration date, nutritional information)

This list doesn't cover everything, and while some sellers choose to include all the information above, others may prefer a more minimalist approach. You might also want to include a story or information about you and the company that helps the customer connect with your brand.

Take, for example, a seller of handcrafted candles who describes her brand as feminine and romantic, using high-quality, eco-friendly ingredients. How can she communicate this in her packaging? To reflect the brand's quality, she might place the candle in a nice glass holder, pack it in a sturdy box closed with a wax seal, and hang a letterpress-printed tag on it. To emphasize the eco-friendly angle, the container could be made of recycled material or the hangtag printed on 100 percent tree-free paper. Graphically, floral motifs, soft borders and colors, or ribbons and tissues in muted colors may suggest the romantic aspect.

You will also need to consider how your products are being sold. Do you sell to retailers who will then display your wares in their store amid a sea of similar products? Do you sell exclusively on your own website? Or do you sell directly to your customers at craft fairs and trunk shows? All of these factors will impact your final decisions in how you want to differentiate your brand through packaging. I will discuss these considerations in more depth in Section 2, where other crafters and I will walk you through choosing the right packaging for your product, taking into account its unique features, any transport and storage requirements, and sales channels.

Your product's packaging is an opportunity for you to connect with your customers. It is your chance to create a memorable impact so that people associate certain attributes with your brand. The experience of holding a nicely packaged product in your hand is very powerful, so don't be afraid to leverage it to your advantage!

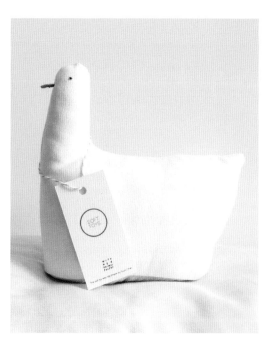

And while we are talking about that customer connection, one other key point to mention: Never forget your target audience! For instance, if your main client base will be affluent fashionistas, they may expect to see products packaged in something a little slicker-looking than kraft paper! Conversely, if your target base is the eco-friendly shopper, they will be dismayed to see products packaged in 100 percent virgin paper, or non-recycled plastic or cotton, and it may even put them off altogether.

Always keep in mind who your customer will be and why they might be buying your product, then use this to create packaging that you think will help add to this appeal. Successful packaging is ultimately a three-way process: what works for you, what works for your product, and what works for your customer.

Opposite: Paper gift tag by Furze Chan, With Her Animal Poetry.
This page: Glass jars with washi tape by Beatriz Gaspar, Con Botas de Agua.

MATERIALS AND HOW TO USE THEM

From paper and fabric to plastic, glass, and recycled materials, there is a myriad of options to meet your packaging needs. Some materials are more familiar than others—who hasn't folded up a piece of paper to make a card or a gift tag?

Other things, on the other hand, might require more practice, such as etching on glass. Remember to keep an open mind and you'll be pleasantly surprised by all the new ideas that spring from experimenting with different materials and techniques.

MATERIALS AND HOW TO USE THEM

PAPER

Paper is one of the most common and versatile packaging materials. It's easy to manipulate, economical, familiar, and widely available, and there are now lots of eco-friendly options. When reflecting on the kind of paper that would suit your product, first consider how you plan to use it: as the core packaging material, to enhance your presentation, or to protect your product during shipping? Also think about the type of paper, its weight, and its thickness.

TYPES OF PAPER

Paper types run the gamut from newsprint and corrugated cardboard to specialty handmade papers. Below is a list of paper options divided into categories that I feel are most relevant in terms of packaging. It's not a complete list, but it should be a great starting point.

WRITING AND DRAWING PAPERS
This group encompasses stationery and artists' papers. Examples include newsprint, notebook and ledger paper, card stock such as construction and cartridge paper, and cotton rag papers.

HANDMADE AND SPECIALTY PAPERS
Made from a diluted mixture of fibers (such as bark, cotton, and bamboo), handmade papers offer a wonderful array of textures. Specialty papers are not always handmade, but include unique materials, such as banana fiber, bamboo, or silk. Examples include Nepalese lokta (rice) papers, mulberry or kozo papers, and Japanese washi paper.

COMMERCIALLY PRINTED PAPERS
These are papers with graphics and text printed on them. Examples include gift-wrap, scrapbooking and origami papers, newspapers, cards, tags, etc.

UTILITARIAN OR INDUSTRIAL PAPERS
This category includes papers commonly used for protecting and shipping products. They may also contain pertinent product information, such as "fragile" or "do not bend." Examples include kraft, butcher, or tissue paper, and corrugated cardboard.

Previous page: Felt flower embellishments by Gemma Behrens, Jac Whippet.
Opposite: Paper treat bags by Danie Pout, BLANK.
This page: Recycled paper tags tied with string by Leonie Cheung, Papercookie.

PAPER AND SUSTAINABILITY

As sustainability has become increasingly important, manufacturers have responded with a variety of eco-friendly papers. If your product itself is eco-friendly, it makes sense to package it with a sustainable material. But when a paper stock is referred to as "green," what does that really mean?

RECYCLED PAPER

This is when waste paper is turned into new paper products. The waste paper is broken down into pulp using water, heat, and chemicals. The pulp mixture is then strained to remove any remaining ink or glue before being made into new paper. Some recycled papers contain BPA (bisphenol A), a potentially harmful chemical that gets into the supply chain through the recycling of thermal papers used for checkout receipts (see resources *p.165* for more information). So you may want to research different paper suppliers and their product ingredients further before making your choice.

This page: Various types of recycled papers.
Opposite: Book made from tree-free paper.

TREE-FREE PAPER

These are papers that are not made of wood pulp. Instead they're made with plant and agricultural fibers, such as bamboo, sugar-cane husk, banana, coffee, straw, or sisal. Cotton and linen papers are great choices for writing and packaging materials due to their luxurious softness. Hemp and jute papers are also gaining popularity because of their beautiful textures and natural colors. Some plant-based papers even have seeds embedded in them so you can plant the paper when you're done with it and watch it grow!

SOY-BASED INKS

As opposed to traditional (petroleum-based) inks, soy-based or vegetable-based inks do not contain petroleum and release less-volatile organic compounds (VOCs) into the atmosphere. Different types of paper take differently to inks, so be sure to test the combination before making a decision, or ask your printer for samples or proofs on the paper stock you are thinking of using.

TIP

The term "paper weight" and the corresponding number refer to the thickness and sturdiness of the paper, not the actual weight of the sheet. This is why the same "weight" paper may be referred to as two different things. For instance, regular copy paper is most commonly referred to as "20-lb bond," but you might also hear it called "60-lb text weight."

Don't worry too much about these technicalities; instead consider the function the paper has to serve. For example, if the paper needs to contain your product, it will need to be sturdy and strong (high-density). If you're going to wrap the paper around your product, it will need to be lightweight and flexible enough. Always test a paper type with a mock-up before you buy. You'll want to be sure the thickness and weight are appropriate for your needs.

USES OF PAPER

BAGS

If you sell directly to your customer, a paper bag can add a nice finishing touch to your presentation. With a little bit of creativity you can elevate even the humble brown paper bag to a chic packaging option for your product. Here we explore the different ways of differentiating your brand using paper bags.

PRE-PRINTED BAGS WITH STICKERS OR LABELS

You can transform a solid-colored paper bag into a really attractive product package by simply adding a wraparound sticker with your brand and product information. Or another option is to pre-print the information directly onto the bag. That way, you can print large quantities and not have to think too much about any further packaging requirements. Other ways of embellishing include hand-stamping and stenciling.

TIP

A lot of people reuse bags, so whenever possible, select good-quality, durable materials.

SEE ALSO Block printing: *pp.66–67*

This page: Kraft bags and fabric tapes by Kat Miller, Cardinal House.
Opposite top: Glassine bags with paper sticker fastening by Danie Pout, BLANK.
Opposite bottom: Bag with detachable hangers by DEDE DextrousDesign.

SEE-THROUGH BAGS

If it is important for your customer to see the product prior to purchase, consider using a paper bag with a transparent glassine window. This is also a good way for customers to differentiate between flavors, types, or styles. Plus, it can be economical: if customers can see the product, you may not need to do separate print runs for each different variety. They're also ideal for showing off brightly colored or uniquely shaped products.

REUSABLE BAGS

The front of your bag presents a great opportunity to showcase your brand. You can experiment with illustrations and graphics that relate to your product or brand. It's a good idea to keep the design consistent as, over time, customers will begin to associate certain visual cues, such as color or graphics, with your brand identity.

BEYOND THE RECTANGULAR BAG

How about thinking outside of the box (or bag in this case) and experimenting with different shapes and structures? This bag, for example, is a fun twist on the regular bag template and also has a detachable coat hanger feature.

BOXES

Boxes are some of the most commonly used types of packaging, and they are readily available in a wide variety of sizes, weights, and colors. The box is a great packaging option for all kinds of things: soft goods, bags, paper products, jewelry, books, art, etc.

HAND-EMBELLISHED VERSUS PRE-PRINTED BOXES

Think about the number of boxes you will need as well as how you'll design them. If you sell an average of three high-priced items a month, then you might consider hand-illustrating each box or using specialty papers for a custom design. If you sell hundreds of units per month, however, a labor-intensive design may not be your best choice. Instead, consider pre-printing your box with the brand's basic graphics and key information, like company name, website, and mission statement, for example.

This page: Printed kraft box by Christopher MacManus, Bittle & Burley.
Opposite top: Mini kraft boxes with washi tape by Danie Pout, BLANK.
Opposite bottom: Printed label by Grace Kang, Olive Box.

SHAPED BOXES AND SPECIAL DIE-CUTS

If you decide to go with pre-printed boxes, consider taking it one step further and designing a signature box that is true to your brand. For instance, if you make and sell honey, perhaps your box could be a hexagon shape instead of rectangular. Or, if you are known for a signature print or pattern on your houseware products, you could feature that pattern on your box.

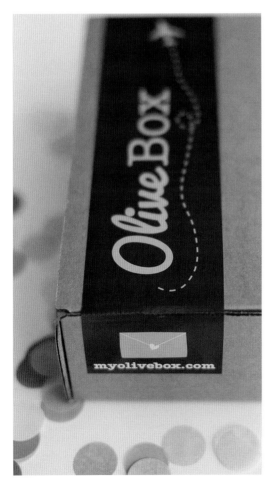

STURDINESS AND WEIGHT

If your products are light, a box made of cardstock might be sufficient, but for heavier goods, you should probably opt for cardboard boxes. In fact, if you are shipping mostly mail orders, you might consider combining your product packaging with your shipping box—an eco-friendly, cost-effective packaging solution. You can always customize a standard cardboard box by hand-printing or embellishing it with your brand stickers.

TIPS

Hand-printed boxes are best used for custom items such as high-end jewelry, one-of-a-kind art pieces, ceramics, and sculpture. Pre-printed boxes are a good idea for high-volume orders.

Fragile products usually call for heavier-weight packaging, which can be more expensive. Remember to factor this into your shipping costs.

SEE ALSO   Templates: pp.166–67
Printing and embellishing
techniques: p.29

WRAPS

Paper wraps range from translucent tissue papers and patterned gift-wraps to sturdy cardboard stock. Wraps work well for both soft and hard goods, and they can cover any amount of the package. Full wraps may cover the entire product, bellybands reveal part of it, or a thin strip of paper tape makes a great accent.

STORE-BOUGHT WRAPS

The difference between wrapping a gift with store-bought paper versus a professionally packaged product is really in the brand identity. After all, without the brand name and product information panel, it would merely be a wrapped object. If you decide to use store-bought paper wraps, make sure to brand the rest of the package with your brand identity and product information. If you have the means, you can go a step further and invest in professionally printed custom wrap emblazoned with your logo or brand name. There are many companies now offering this service, but naturally it will cost more.

TIPS

Unlikely paper sources such as newspapers, book pages, and scrapbooking papers can make charming packaging materials.

Thin papers are best used for lightweight and dry products, such as jewelry, light clothing, and accessories. Stickers, tape, and string are all good techniques for sealing thin papers.

 Printing and embellishing techniques: *p.29*

HAND-PRINTED WRAPS

Certain products and types of paper are naturally suited to one another. For instance, greaseproof wax paper is an obvious choice for baked goods. That said, the type of paper your wrap is made from will determine how to embellish it. For example, thin papers are hard to stencil because they tear easily.

ADHESIVE WRAPS (PAPER TAPE)

Adhesive tapes such as kraft and metallic foil tapes are great as they both seal the package and add a decorative accent. The ever-popular washi paper tape presents many possibilities as it comes in a rainbow of colors and patterns. Or, you can pre-print your brand identity on regular tape.

BELLYBANDS

If you are bundling products, a bellyband is a great option. With lightweight, smaller objects such as a series of cards or prints, you really only need a light- to medium-weight bellyband. If you are putting a bellyband around a box, however, you might consider a heavier paper stock, such as cardboard. Ensure the bellyband fits around the product snugly but is not so tight that it becomes difficult to remove.

Opposite: Letterpress-printed tags and printed wraps by Alischa Herrmann, Bespoke Letterpress.
This page top: Divine Dairy cheese wrap by Frank Aloi Design Co.
This page bottom: Kraft paper bellyband by Amber Corcoran, Fancy Tiger Crafts.

23

TAGS AND LABELS

If the packaging you use is difficult to print on, you can still brand your products by adding hangtags and labels. They're also a simple and effective way to accent your packaging and distinguish your brand. As hangtags do not need to fit the dimensions of each product, they have the added perk of minimizing your packaging costs.

PRE-PRINTED HANGTAGS

If you regularly have large orders, pre-printed hangtags can be a real life-saver, especially if the same artwork appears consistently across your different product styles. You can print the tags in large sheets of card stock and cut them down to size, or print on pre-cut tags. If you only need a generic brand tag, consider using your hangtag as your business card as well. As quantities increase, the per-unit cost of each piece goes down.

DIE-CUTS AND SPECIALTY-PRINTED TAGS AND LABELS

Maybe your hangtag is the one element you decide to splurge on. If you opt to go all out and foil-stamp your tags, also consider designing them in different shapes, or using luxurious printmaking papers.

This page top: Letterpress-printed tags by Alischa Herrmann, Bespoke Letterpress.
This page bottom: Die-cut hangtags by Brittni Mehlhoff, Paper & Stitch.
Opposite top: Waterproof polymer labels by Stacie Humpherys, Girl*In*Gear Studio.
Opposite bottom: Handmade hangtags by Danie Pout, BLANK.

WRAPAROUND LABELS AND STICKERS

Adhesive labels are ideal, not just for displaying product information but also for sealing the package. For instance, wraparound labels for tubes or boxes and stickers on tissue paper act as sealants to protect the package. They work well for wines, jams, sauces, bath and beauty products, and most products housed in boxes and bags.

HANDMADE HANGTAGS

When making your handmade tags, remember that the little details make them special: adding a grommet in your brand color to support the hole where the string goes, rounding the tag corners, adding scalloped edges, or stringing the tag with distinctive ribbons, for example. You can create the artwork on your computer and print the tags on thick card stock, or you can hand-print on premade or hand-cut tags. You can also get reasonably priced paper punches in craft stores, specifically for making hangtags that come in a range of shapes. And even better—you can use them again and again, and they won't break the bank. To help get you started, a range of templates for tags has been included in the resources section of this book.

TIP

If you embellish your tags one piece at a time, why not experiment with specialty paper stocks, such as bamboo or silk paper, or industrial ones like manila and circle tags?

FILLING AND PADDING

Internal filling and padding is just as important as the external appearance of your packaging. These materials protect your products as they are stored or transported from place to place, and well-protected products that arrive safely with the customer will increase trust in your brand.

WRAPPING PAPERS

Lightweight papers such as tissue, newsprint, butcher paper, and kraft are extremely versatile wrapping and padding options. Butcher paper is great for food products and perishables, while tissues and newsprint work well for wrapping all kinds of products, as well as for cushioning and filling the gaps in your box. Kraft paper is stronger than newsprint, making it more suitable for wrapping heavier objects like paintings and sculptures. Polycoated kraft is a heavyweight version often used to wrap metal parts and keep products dry. Most of these papers are biodegradable and compostable.

CORRUGATED PADS

Corrugated pads are made up of layers of corrugated and laminated sheets, and they can be cut into specific sizes according to your needs. They're most commonly used to top-layer cartons and boxes, protecting the contents from box-cutter and knife blades, and to protect the products from dust during storage. Being flexible and easy to bend, corrugated pads can work well for a lot of other products too, especially large items like oversized art pieces or furniture.

EDGE AND CORNER PROTECTORS

Corner protectors are essential when shipping paintings, art prints, frames, and furniture. They come in a variety of sizes and shapes to ensure minimal shuffling during transportation and protect items from dents and scratches. They are usually made from strong cardboard but are also available in plastic, foam, and wood.

CUSHIONING MATERIALS

Shredded newsprint (sold in bulk), eco-friendly honeycomb-padded paper backed with tissue, and kraft strands are all good substitutes for bubble wrap and work well for cushioning all kinds of products. I am partial to the honeycombed products because they provide protection with less weight and waste, and they are biodegradable. Padded mailers are considered ready-to-mail; they don't require any additional packaging or padding, so they're ideal for smaller items like CDs, beauty products, and little art pieces. Most of these cushioning materials are recyclable.

Opposite: Newsprint wrap for wine bottles by Glenn Grech, and Karl Attard, BRND WGN.
Top left: Corrugated packing sheets.
Top right: Kraft box and crinkle paper cushions by Andrew Payne, General Knot & Co.

PRINTING AND EMBELLISHING TECHNIQUES

PRINTING OPTIONS

Now that you have an understanding of the types of paper available, let's look at the options for printing and embellishing it.

PROFESSIONAL PRINTING

Professional printing is simply any printing you pay another firm to do for you, as opposed to doing it yourself. There are a couple of different types of professional printing you might consider:

Offset: Offset (or lithographic) printing involves creating a set of "plates" from which the image is pressed onto paper. The setup costs are higher than for other printing techniques, but it's worth it for long print runs because the finished product looks great. Luxury packaging is usually offset-printed and UV-coated for long-term protection.

Digital: Digital printing is basically a "print straight from the computer" method. The turnaround time is faster and it's more economical for short print runs. In recent years, the quality of digital printing has really improved, giving offset printing a run for its money.

SPECIALTY PRINTING

The following printing methods utilize special equipment and presses, and tend to cost more than the basic methods, but they offer subtly unique looks that can really make your packaging stand out.

Foil Stamping: Foil stamping relies on pressure to create an image, using foil film instead of inks. This results in less color variance across different papers. Foils are especially effective for metallic finishes or when applying light colors to a darker base.

Engraving: Similarly, engraving also imposes an image onto paper under intense pressure, but the effect is a raised image on paper. Due to its premium pricing and its elegant look, engraving is often reserved for formal pieces only.

Thermography: Thermography is similar to engraving, but it relies on heat instead of pressure to create images and it is less expensive.

Letterpress: Letterpress is a relief-printing method where the raised, inked image meets the paper and makes an indentation. The result is tactile and lovely, and a very popular option for high-end stationery and packaging.

This page: Letterpress card by Viola E. Sutanto, Chewing the Cud.
Opposite: Handmade rubber stamp by Gemma Behrens, Jac Whippet.

HAND-PRINTING

Hand-printing naturally conveys a more customized, homemade feel that can also project your own personality. I love hand-printing for many reasons: The setup is usually more economical as it doesn't require any big machinery or special expertise. The experience is fun because you get to experiment with different kinds of artwork!

Stamping/Block Printing: If you are a beginner, I would suggest starting with hand-stamping as it has the simplest setup. All you need is a store-bought or hand-carved stamp and an inkpad, and you're ready to go! Block printing is similar in that the artwork is carved from a wood or linoleum block and ink is applied before stamping onto the surface.

Stenciling: Stenciling is a resist technique, meaning that you block out all the parts you don't want printed. You carve the artwork on a stiff material (such as cardboard or plastic) and place it on top of the paper, and then apply ink. This technique is especially appropriate for bold, graphic designs.

Silk Screen: If you are looking to create very detailed art with consistent results, silk-screen printing might be the way to go. It does require a more extensive setup, but once you do all the prep work it's easy to reproduce the art on as many pieces as you like.

TIP
Note that these printing techniques can be applied to other materials, in addition to paper. Always remember to test-print using scrap materials before you begin to print.

SEE ALSO Block printing: pp.66–67

TUTORIALS

PAPER-CUTTING

The presence of a customized hangtag can transform a generic brown cardboard box into a simple yet effective packaging solution. In this case, a paper-cut illustration enhances the brand identity, while the box can package a variety of products.

BRAND
Rosefinch Bath

BRAND ATTRIBUTES
Natural. Handmade. Joyful. Peaceful. Serene.

PRODUCTS
Lotions, balms, bar soaps, oils

PACKAGING NOTES
The rosefinch has a visually pleasing appearance that makes it a symbolic icon for the brand—the products suggest an experience of relaxation and tranquility that enriches the senses. Being produced in small batches by hand, it seemed fitting that the hangtags should also be paper-cut individually. As the products come in various shapes and sizes, it is important that the packaging can accommodate single or multiple items. Therefore, we decided generic boxes with a paper-cut, branded hangtag as the unifying element would be the most appropriate format.

Materials used

- HANGTAGS
- PENCIL
- TRACING PAPER
- BONE FOLDER OR SMALL SPOON
- UTILITY/CRAFT KNIFE WITH A SHARP BLADE
- CUTTING MAT (OR HEAVY CARDBOARD AS CUTTING SURFACE)
- STRING, TWINE, OR RIBBON

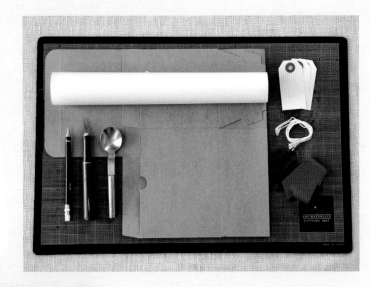

1 Use tracing paper to copy the chosen artwork. Alternatively, you can draw directly onto the hangtag.

2 Turn the tracing paper over and place onto your hangtag.

3 Using your spoon or bone folder, rub down carefully but fairly vigorously so that the graphite from the pencil transfers the artwork to the hangtag.

4 With your knife, carefully cut around the shape of the artwork. When the entire image is cut through, gently press to release the cut portion from the hangtag.

TIP
When cutting certain shapes, like curves, try slowly moving the hangtag itself as well as the knife in the cutting motion, for a smoother line and finish.

SEE ALSO

Image transfer: *pp.32–33*
Block printing: *pp.66–67*

IMAGE TRANSFER

This project is an easy and economical way of transferring images onto paper using either a solvent or a household cleaning product such as Citra Solv. You can use this method for lots of different surfaces, but for this project we'll transfer images onto paper that we'll then use to wrap a product.

BRAND
Drawn by Emma

BRAND ATTRIBUTES
One-of-a-kind. Precious. Nostalgic.

PRODUCTS
Custom portraits

PACKAGING NOTES
Drawn by Emma is a company that creates custom portraits from photographs. These photographs are often from the long-distant past, so they have a nostalgic feel to them. Each portrait is a one-of-a-kind art piece, so we wanted the packaging to communicate that uniqueness.

Materials used

- SOLVENT
- COTTON BALLS
- PHOTOCOPIES OF IMAGES
- BONE FOLDER OR SPOON
- PAPER
- TAPE

1 Make some photocopies of the image(s) you would like to use, or print them from a toner-based (not solid ink) laser printer. Believe it or not, the older the printer or copier, the better.

2 Place the photocopy face down onto the printing surface. Carefully apply your chosen solvent to the back of the paper and rub (always ensure the area you are working in is properly ventilated when using solvents and read any safety advice on the packaging). Use your spoon or bone folder for more pressure.

3 Carefully lift up one corner of the photocopy to see if you're happy with the transfer. If not, continue to rub with your spoon to release the liquid toner (melted by the solvent) onto the paper.

4 Voila! You have a one-of-a-kind paper wrap for your product. Feel free to get creative and paint or draw on your transfer!

TIP

Single-color images generally work best. The transferred image is a reversal of the original, so if there is text, be sure to flip the image.

MATERIALS AND HOW TO USE THEM

PLASTIC

Plastic is one of the most versatile packaging materials around. It molds to all shapes and sizes, it's robust, and it usually has a smooth surface, so you can easily apply adhesive or ink to it. Well suited to printing and embellishing, you have a wide range of design options available, both commercially and DIY. Plastic's light but durable quality is ideal for transporting products and protecting them from damage and leaking. Lighter-weight packaging also means less fuel consumption for shipping. Finally, some plastics can be completely sealed, and that makes them perfect for keeping foods fresh and uncontaminated. Contrary to its bad reputation, many plastics are actually recyclable.

TYPES OF PLASTIC

Most of us are familiar with the Society of the Plastics Industry's (SPI) recycling symbol —a single digit (1–7) surrounded by a triangle of arrows. Each category is defined by its make, density, melting point, degree of safety for consumers, and ease of recycling. The seven types of plastic are described below.

PET (POLYETHYLENE TEREPHTHALATE)
PET is used to make bottles for beverages and mouthwash. It's generally safe and is recyclable.

HDPE (HIGH-DENSITY POLYETHYLENE)
HDPE is used for milk, detergent, and oil bottles. It's mostly opaque and is easily recyclable.

PVC (POLYVINYL CHLORIDE)
PVC uses include food packaging and blister packs. It is durable but a challenge to recycle.

LDPE (LOW-DENSITY POLYETHYLENE)
LDPE is used to make squeezable bottles and frozen food bags. It is safe but not easy to recycle.

PP (POLYPROPYLENE)
PP is used to make margarine and yogurt containers. It is considered safe and is generally recyclable.

PS (POLYSTYRENE)
PS is used for fast food trays. PS may release toxic chemicals when heated and is hard to recycle.

OTHER
The 7 code indicates that the item is made either with a resin other than the six listed above or with a combination of different resins.

Opposite: Cello bag with printed tag by Rosemary Gutierrez, Paper Beats Rock.
This page: Plastic pint containers with paper sleeves by 1 Trick Pony.

USES OF PLASTIC

BAGS AND BOXES

Plastic boxes come in a wide range of sizes and shapes, including pillow, oval and hexagon boxes, and gable-style. They also come with both hinged and lift-off lids as well as a variety of handles and effects. Plastic bags also come in an assortment of finishes, from clear or frosted to opaque matte and with or without handles.

PRE-PRINTED BOXES, BAGS, AND PAILS

If you are an established seller or have a large product selection, you might consider pre-printed plastic packaging. There are a couple of ways to accomplish this: printing directly on the box, or printing on paper and applying that to the packaging. Since most plastic packaging is translucent or clear, you really don't need a lot of printing on the box. In fact, you'll probably want to avoid obscuring the contents with lots of printing so that you can really showcase your product.

TIPS

Lightweight poly bags are ideal for small items such as jewelry, baked goods, accessories, clothing, cards, and zines.

Pre-printed plastic bags and boxes suit a wide array of products and are ideal for high-volume sellers.

This page: Pre-printed label design by Dovile Klepaciute, Lushleys Ltd; plastic box by Meridian SP Ltd.
Opposite top: Cardboard backing for brooch in cellophane sleeve by Verónica de Arriba, Depeapa.
Opposite bottom: Tyvek drawstring bag by Katerina Sachova, Papelote.

POLY BAGS

Poly bags come in a wide range of weights, sizes, and types: flat, gusseted (expandable), self-sealing, resealable, zippered, and so forth. Different grades are assigned to poly bags based on their density, so be sure to test your product in some samples before buying bags in bulk. If you are using them to package food products, check to make sure the bag is food-safe.

FOAM BOXES

Not all foam is evil. Some foam boxes are actually recyclable and are certainly reusable. Foam boxes are ideal for packaging foods from pies and cakes to poultry, perishables, and any kind of temperature-sensitive product.

TYVEK

Tyvek is a recyclable material made from high-density polyethylene fibers. Many embellishment techniques can be applied to it, including printing, lamination, embossing, grommeting, and sewing. It is flexible like fabric, but it's particularly resistant to tears and moisture. Tyvek envelopes and bags work for all types of goods, from paper to metal products.

BOTTLES

When selecting your bottle, remember the packaging has to be "fit for purpose." That means it should hold and protect your product well, and keep it safe from damage or contamination.

PRE-PRINTED BOTTLES

As discussed earlier in the chapter, there are many ways of printing on plastic, such as screen printing and foil stamping, or applying decals and labels. If you decide to pre-print your bottles, be sure to research the appropriate printing method for your type of bottle and the kind of use it will see. Bottled products are often used over time, for example, so factors like water-resistance and durability are especially important.

TIP
Pre-printed bottles are ideal for sauces, honey, juices, and spices, and beauty products such as lotions and fragrances.

This page: Silk-screen-printed label by Jamie Jones, Mrs. Jones' Soapbox.
Opposite top: Digitally printed kraft label by Stacie Humpherys, Girl*In*Gear Studio.
Opposite bottom: Thermal-printed labels by Liz Cook, One Seed.

SPECIAL FEATURES

Think about any special features required for your bottle packaging: Does your product require a wide rim for easy scooping? Perhaps you make lotions that require a pump dispenser top. Maybe your fragrances are best packaged in a spritzer bottle. Does the bottle need to be food-safe? You might even decide to forgo the bottle altogether and opt for jars, canisters, or vials instead.

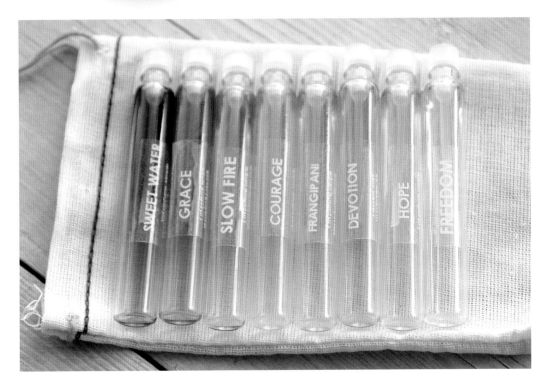

STORE-BOUGHT BOTTLES WITH ADHESIVE LABELS

With blank store-bought bottles, you can customize your labels and run them through your home printer. This is a pretty easy way to package products with multiple flavors and styles, such as sauces, juices, lotions, or spices.

TAGS, WRAPS, AND TAPE

The biggest advantage of using plastic tags, wraps, and tape for packaging is their durability and resistance to moisture. That makes them a popular option for foods and perishables.

TAGS

Pre-printed plastic hangtags are generally more costly to produce than paper tags, but they won't tear and they're water-resistant, plus they can be embossed or screen printed for a professional look. Plastic tags are ideal for higher-priced items, or for products that are likely to be exposed to dirt and moisture.

WRAPS

Plastic wraps are generally used for sealing food, and they come in clear sheets or rolls. They can be challenging to hand-print on, so embellishing with stickers or tape is a more viable option. Clear or printed shrink-wrap is a common way to bundle multiple products and is a great method for allowing the products to remain visible. Wraparound labels are adhered around the product, and they're most popularly used to label bottles and jars.

TAPE

While commonly used as sealants, polyethylene or plastic tape can also make a fun addition to your packaging as a finishing touch or to bundle light products together. You can choose from a wide variety of sizes, colors, and patterns. If you want the tape to double up as a sealant, be sure to pick one that is appropriate for your product weight. Alternatively, you can choose to custom-print your own plastic tape.

TIPS

Pre-printed wraps are best for high-volume orders, while wraparound labels are mostly used for wine, sauce, spices, bath and beauty products, and other items that are handled frequently.

Custom-printed tape is a practical packaging solution for high-volume sellers.

Opposite: Dry-erase and chalkboard tags by Natalie Jost, Olive Manna.
This page top: Divine Dairy cheese wrap by Frank Aloi Design Co.
This page bottom: Screen-printed, patterned tape by Caramela; design by Lucía Elizondo, Anagrama.

FILLING, PADDING, AND WRAPS

Plastic materials make great void fillers and padding for packaging because they are very lightweight, moisture-resistant, and they keep food products fresh for an extended period. Below are some options for your consideration.

CELLOPHANE AND CLING WRAP

Plastic wraps are typically sold in rolls. Cling wrap can stretch over smooth surfaces, staying tightly in place over itself or a container without adhesive. It is ideal for food products because it keeps them dry and fresh. Luckily for us, there are now some eco-friendly cling-wrap products that are also biodegradable. Similarly, commercial shrink wrap is self-sticking, and it's good for securing products together. Clear and colored cellophane wrap work really well with confectionery as well as some bath products such as bath bombs.

This page: Cello bag by Rachel Ball, Mignon Kitchen Co.
Opposite: Assorted types of plastic filling and cushioning material.

BUBBLE WRAP

Bubble wrap can be used as a buffer between products, or you can wrap it around individual items for protection. Bubble wrap is available with bubbles of different sizes, depending on the size of the object being packed and the amount of cushioning needed. Eco-friendly bubble wrap is 100 percent recyclable, biodegradable, and CFC-free, which means it does not deplete the ozone layer.

PEANUTS

Also known as loose fill, peanuts are used to fill in any spaces around the product to cushion it on all sides. It is very lightweight, which helps you save on shipping costs. Instead of the polystyrene type, you can use biodegradable peanuts, made from vegetable starch, which are water-soluble and also compostable.

AIR PILLOWS

Air pillows can be purchased in rolls, although they are usually not prefilled with air so you will also need to buy the corresponding air-cushion machine. Recyclable options are available too. What I love about air pillows is how light they are, and customers can unpack their box without any of the mess associated with other fillings like peanuts.

TIP

Peanuts, bubble wrap, and air pillows are all great for protecting fragile items such as glass, ceramics, sculpture, and art pieces.

PRINTING AND EMBELLISHING TECHNIQUES

MAKING LABELS

Some of the printing techniques described in the Paper chapter (pages 28–29), such as screen printing, digital printing, and foil stamping, can also be applied to plastics. Other techniques, however, such as heat transfers and pressure-sensitive labeling are applied more exclusively to plastics.

HEAT-TRANSFER DECALS
A heat-transfer decal is a high-quality digitally printed or screen-printed image on a clear surface (much like a sticker) that is permanently bonded to a surface using heat and pressure. They can be applied to a variety of plastic materials, such as polypropylene, polyethylene, PVC, and acrylic. And of course, if the decals are pre-printed, you are not restricted to using just one color as you might be with other DIY methods (like hand-stamping, for example) and they can be very detailed. Depending on the image size and the number of parts to be decorated, heat-transfer decals can be a cost-effective alternative to other decorating methods.

PRESSURE-SENSITIVE LABELING
Commonly used by the beauty and health industry, this is a type of cylindrical screen printing that applies a label on the front and back of a package (or even a full wraparound) in one pass. This method is especially cost-effective if you are making large quantities.

TIP
Fragile products usually call for heavier-weight packaging, which can be more expensive; remember to factor this into your shipping costs.

HAND-PRINTING: STENCILING AND HAND-ILLUSTRATING

Of the many hand-printing techniques, stenciling is probably one of the most suitable for plastic packaging, since most plastic containers are curved (for example, bottles). Remember to use a flexible material for your template so it can wrap around your packaging structure. See the tutorial on pages 46–47.

CUSTOM ADHESIVE LABELS

If commercially printing on plastics is too expensive an option, you might want to consider purchasing premade plastic containers and creating your own packaging labels. The tutorial on pages 48–49 includes templates (to scan, copy or download) that you can use to start designing your own labels.

Opposite: Plastic tub with silk-screen-printed label by Jamie Jones, Mrs. Jones' Soapbox.
This page: Plastic bottles with adhesive label by The Butter Factory; design by Swear Words.

TUTORIALS

STENCILING WITH CONTACT PAPER

Stenciling is an inexpensive and easy way to ink your images onto plastic. Here we will be creating the stencil template with contact paper because our packaging surface is curved, but you can also use a rigid material such as cardboard or card stock to make a template.

BRAND
Yoo! Chocolates

BRAND ATTRIBUTES
Artisan (handmade). Bold flavors. Fun.

PRODUCTS
Gourmet chocolates

PACKAGING NOTES
Yoo! Chocolates specialize in making artisan chocolates in fun and unique flavors, such as lavender, mint, or rosemary. However, as most of their products look very similar—round and mostly dark brown—it can be hard to distinguish between the flavors. So for the packaging, we thought it would be fun to stencil some bold shapes to highlight the interesting ingredients inside.

Materials used

- PLASTIC CONTAINERS
- CONTACT PAPER (ACETATE OR STENCIL PAPER ALSO WORKS; YOU CAN FIND THESE IN CRAFT STORES AND SOME STATIONERY STORES)
- MARKER OR PENCIL
- UTILITY OR CRAFT KNIFE WITH A SHARP BLADE
- SCREEN-PRINTING INKS
- STENCIL BRUSH
- CUTTING MAT (OR HEAVY CARDBOARD TO USE AS A CUTTING SURFACE)
- PALETTE OR PAPER PLATE

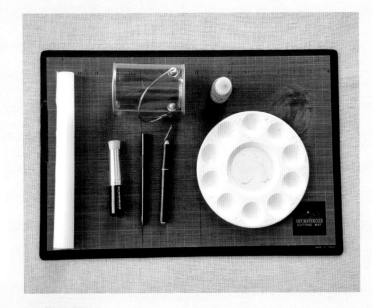

1 Draw or trace your design onto the back of the contact paper. Cut out the design using your knife. Remove the contact paper backing and position it in the desired place on the mini pail.

2 Pour a small amount of ink onto the palette and load the brush with the ink. Now, dab the brush a few times onto some paper towel to remove any excess ink. This is called loading and stippling; it helps to give the design crisp edges. Loading too much ink can cause the ink to seep under the edges of the stencil.

3 Holding the mini pail steady, apply your loaded brush to the open areas of the stencil in a rapid up-and-down movement. Work with small strokes, taking care not to peel off any stencil as you apply. When you're done, let the ink dry before carefully peeling off the stencil.

TIP
Loading and stippling is just one way of applying ink. A sponge is another great method, especially for larger designs.

CREATING CUSTOM LABELS

Instead of printing directly onto plastic, here we will be creating custom labels using the resizable templates provided at the back of the book. Feel free to further embellish the labels or customize them with your brand colors and fonts. Once you're happy with your label, you can print as needed and start applying them to your products!

BRAND
Floria Bath Salts

BRAND ATTRIBUTES
Feminine. Rejuvenating. High quality.

PRODUCTS
Luxury bath salts in various fragrances

PACKAGING NOTES
Currently, Floria carry a line of bath salts in distinctive fragrances and in two sizes: the 1-ounce (20ml) sampler and the 4-ounce (120ml) jar. The packaging needs to not only distinguish between the two sizes but also identify the different scents. To simplify the process, we applied the same design to labels of varying sizes, and used color as a coding system for the fragrances.

Materials used

- PLASTIC JARS AND VIALS
- MEASURING TAPE OR RULER AND STRING
- COMPUTER WITH GRAPHIC-EDITING SOFTWARE
- FULL SHEET ADHESIVE LABELS
- SCISSORS OR SHARP UTILITY KNIFE AND RULER

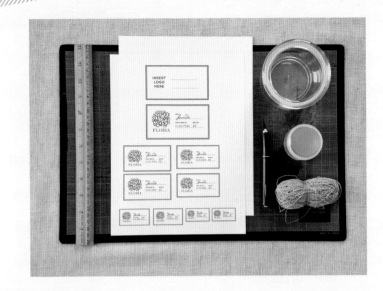

1 After determining the types of jars or bottles you want to use, with your ruler and string measure directly against the container to determine your ideal label size. Then select a sheet of adhesive labels corresponding as closely as possible to that size for your printing needs. Or just print on a full, blank sheet of adhesive paper and trim to size later.

2 Download or scan the label template at the back of the book and resize in your graphic-editing software as appropriate. Once you have your blank template set up correctly, simply add text and image(s) according to your preference.

3 Feed the adhesive label sheet through your printer. Print and trim your labels as needed.

MATERIALS AND HOW TO USE THEM

FABRIC

The major advantage of fabric as a packaging material is its flexibility; you can fold and wrap fabric in any shape or form, and cut it to any size to suit your needs. It's widely available, and you can get all kinds of textures, colors, and patterns, plus there are plenty of eco-friendly options. When used as filling or padding in a box or mailer, fabric provides great product protection.

TYPES OF FABRIC

While there are tons of fabric options out there, I've chosen to list the ones that are the most viable for packaging. The categories below cover a wide range of uses, price points, and most are readily available in stores or online.

LIGHTWEIGHT FABRIC
These types of fabric are widely available in stores in a variety of colors, sizes, and weights. Using light fabrics will often help reduce your overall shipping cost. Examples of lightweight fabrics include cotton, muslin, and linen.

HANDMADE OR SPECIALTY FABRICS
This category consists of those with unusual textures and encompasses fabrics with graphics and text printed on them. Examples include velvet, jute, hemp, and woven or printed fabrics.

UTILITARIAN OR INDUSTRIAL FABRICS
Utilitarian fabrics tend to be heavier-weight, but they are very durable and provide good protection for products. Some are used mainly for outdoor purposes and are usually laminated or waterproofed. Examples include burlap, duck canvas, netting, awning, and sailcloth.

Opposite: Furoshiki wraps by Kyoko Bowskill, LINK.
This page: Assorted fabrics on display at a sewing center.

WORKING WITH ECO-FRIENDLY FABRICS

If you're looking to use eco-friendly fabrics, you'll want to consider how the fibers are grown and manufactured, the sustainability of the farming practices, and how the raw materials and finished fabrics are transported. In a nutshell, you want fabrics that are produced with minimal negative impact on the environment. Here's a quick primer on some key terms for eco-friendly fabrics.

SUSTAINABLE FIBERS

Sustainable fibers come from rapidly renewable resources—those with a short harvest cycle, like bamboo and hemp. Both of these are considered "good guys" because they are easy to grow without pesticides and they grow quickly. Bamboo fabric is soft, beautiful, and can serve a multitude of uses. Hemp is extremely versatile and durable. Both materials can make a wide range of products, such as rope or clothing. While both fabrics convey an eco-friendly message, bamboo is often associated with more high-end products.

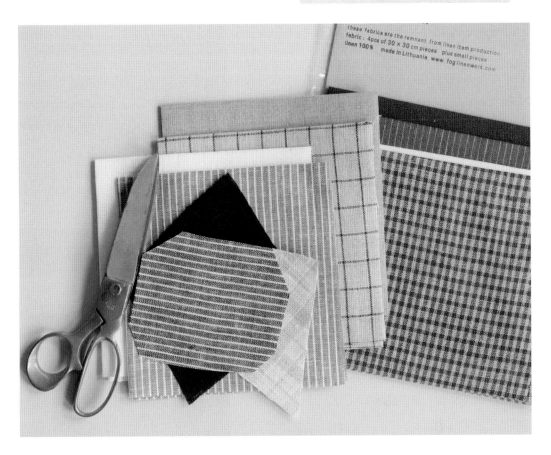

ORGANIC FABRICS

Conventionally grown cotton uses more insecticides than any other crop. Not only do these methods harm the environment, they also create adverse working conditions for the cotton workers.

By definition, organic farming does not use any pesticides, fungicides, herbicides, or artificial fertilizers. Admittedly, the higher cost of organic cotton can be prohibitive, but on a positive note, as demand for it continues to rise, farmers on a global scale are converting from conventional to organic farming practices. Thus organic cotton prices have dropped in recent years.

RECYCLED FABRICS

Recycled fabrics come from post-consumer waste, such as soda bottles, or post-industrial waste (byproducts from the manufacturing process). For instance, recycled cotton is made from combining leftover scraps and excess yarn, shredding it all down into fibers, and spinning it into yarns. The yarns are then woven or knitted into new textiles. Cotton recycling is eco-friendly because it does not use any new cotton, dyes, or harsh chemicals.

Opposite: Hand-printed market bag with kraft card hangtag by Nicole James, Yardage Design.
This page: Linen remnant set by Yumiko Sekine, Fog Linen Work.

USES OF FABRIC

WRAPS

Fabric wrapping is one of the most eco-friendly forms of packaging as it can be reused repeatedly. And, if the fabric itself is recycled or organic, and printed with vegetable-based inks, you get extra brownie points! You can wrap all kinds of things, from small items to awkward shapes. When selecting your fabric, consider how you plan to embellish it, the size you need, the type of material, and overall costs.

STORE-BOUGHT WRAPS

Traditional fabric wraps, or furoshiki, are often made of silk, but modern fabric wraps include chirimen crepe, cotton, and nylon. Select colors and patterns that speak to your product, and use add-ons like hangtags to distinguish your brand. Fabric wraps are ideal for a wide array of products from small and precious pieces to larger items like ceramics, home goods, accessories, clothing, cakes and pies, or dry food products. Most lightweight fabrics will work well for wrapping because they are easy to handle. When wrapping heavy items, I tend to pick stiffer fabrics. If this is your first fabric wrap, I recommend using lightweight cotton as your practice cloth.

This page: Fabric give wraps™ by Viola E. Sutanto, Chewing the Cud.
Opposite top: Furoshiki wrap by Kyoko Bowskill, LINK.
Opposite bottom: Gift seed bundle in vintage fabric by Jen O'Connor, The Little Ragamuffin.

HAND-PRINTED WRAPS

In deciding how to embellish your wrap, think about the type of fabric: Is it a loosely or tightly woven cloth? Fine details on your artwork could get lost in loose-weave fabrics. The color of your wrap might determine the inks you use—certain fabrics don't respond well to certain inks. Also consider how you want to finish your wrap: You could sew the edges, cut them with pinking shears, or keep the threads loose for a more rustic feel.

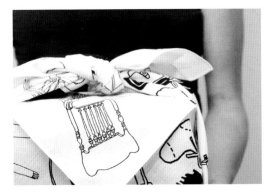

WRAPPING WITH SCRAPS

Wrapping with scrap cloth is both eco-friendly and inexpensive, and can be further embellished if needed. Wrapping with scraps is ideal for small items like jewelry, accessories, or bath and beauty products. It is also a good option if environmental credentials are an important part of your brand.

TIP

Although not an exact science, aim to get the diagonal line of a square piece of fabric about three times as long as the product.

 SEE ALSO Printing and embellishing techniques: *pp.62-63*

BAGS, SACKS, AND ENVELOPES

If the thought of wrapping your objects in fabric makes you want to run for the hills, perhaps fabric bags and sacks are the way to go. Many are available for bulk purchase as "blanks" (unprinted) in stores and online, in a variety of materials, sizes, colors, and weights, and are easy to embellish in any way you choose. Personally, I like to use recycled cotton canvas for its natural color and printability.

SACKS

Another variation on the bag is the fabric sack, which is fastened by tying a ribbon at the top. You can buy blank or printed sacks and customize them using ribbons and strings that reflect your brand. You can even make your own sacks using squares of fabric and string or ribbon.

ENVELOPES

Experiment with different fabrics and make envelopes by cutting the fabric to size, folding it over, and stitching the sides. Fabric envelopes are an ideal packaging option for jewelry, accessories, and small, flat goods.

SPECIALTY BAGS AND TOTES

Totes and drawstring bags come in a variety of materials—cotton, linen, burlap, to name a few. Some bags are specifically made for certain products. These include wine bottle totes, gusseted cake bags, burlap bags for coffee and rice, and mesh produce bags.

SACHETS

Small cotton or muslin sachets are adorable and easy to print on due to their smaller, flat surfaces. If you use them for food products, make sure you purchase a food-safe variety. If you are handy with a sewing machine, consider truly personalizing your fabric packaging by sewing your own sachets.

TIPS

Sachets are ideal for very small items such as jewelry and accessories, candy, chocolates, and small baked goods.

Totes are great for smaller to mid-sized items, but fragile objects should be separated. This option is ideal for a wide array of products, but especially useful for oddly shaped things such as ceramic or glass pieces and sculptures.

SEE ALSO Resources: *pp. 170-71*

Opposite: Herb bundles in vintage napkin sachets by Jen O'Connor, The Little Ragamuffin.
This page: Linen jewelry pouch by Alessandra Taccia, Knots.

RIBBONS, TAPE, AND TIES

Whether your overall package is made of fabric or a combination of different materials, fabric enclosures are a charming way to add the finishing touch to your packaging. From ribbons and string ties to tape, the possibilities are endless. As the saying goes, it's all in the details!

RIBBONS

There are so many ribbon types on the market: brocade, silk, satin, sheer, velvet, grosgain, organza, linen, rayon, and polyester, not to mention the myriad of colors and designs available. When selecting your ribbon, consider how you want it to complement your brand packaging. Hand-dyed silk ribbons convey a sophisticated, high-end look; grosgrain has a preppy, streamlined appearance; while linen brings to mind a simple, natural feel. Width matters too: Thinner ribbons or those delicate in design are more suited to smaller items, while bulkier packages warrant a wider ribbon.

TAPE

Taping your package with fabric adds a lovely texture and surprise element to it. It softens the look of the overall package, especially against a harder material such as wood or metal. Most fabric tapes are lightweight, so if your tape has to serve the dual purpose of decorating and sealing your package securely, be sure to apply a heavier paper or plastic tape first, and layer the fabric tape on top of it.

TIES

This category covers all types of string: hemp twine, raffia, baker's twine, cording, trimmings, yarn, and dyed threads and tassels, to name a few. Beyond the look and feel, be mindful of the durability and strength of these ties when making your selection. Hemp, for example, is extremely sturdy, so it's best used for heavyweight products, while baker's twine is lightweight and pairs well with a small, delicate package or hangtag.

TIP
Fabric tape is better suited to smaller products and packages that don't need the heavy-duty support of packaging tape.

Opposite top: Fabric bundles tied with ribbon.
Opposite bottom: Linen tape by Yumiko Sekine, Fog Linen Work.
This page: Fabric cords and trims can be used as colorful fabric ties.

FILLING AND PADDING

Fabric padding is not as lightweight as paper or plastic, so it could end up costing more in shipping. It's still a viable option, though, because of its ability to protect fragile or precious objects against scratches, dust, and dents.

FABRIC PADS AND LINERS

Flat fabric sheets are sometimes used to protect expensive products like paintings during transit. Felt or lint-free cloth is widely used for this purpose because it provides good padding and protection against scratches and dust. Felt and cotton pads can also also be cut to size and used to line small jewelry boxes.

BATTING AND STUFFING

Batting (also known as wadding) is the layer of insulation that's found between the two pieces of fabric in a quilt. It is usually made of polyester, cotton, or bamboo fibers, and it's lightweight enough that you can use it as padding or filler in your packaging.

TIPS

Fabric liners are great for glass, art, sculpture, silverware and soft metals, and jewelry.

Batting is ideal for more fragile products that need additional protection against scratches and dents.

This page: Batting material.
Opposite: Different types of fabric.

FABRIC SCRAPS

Shredded fabric scraps provide good cushioning for fragile items, but they are heavier than paper or plastic filler and therefore less cost-effective. Unless you already have fabric scraps lying around that are ready to use as filler, I would recommend using air pillows or honeycombed paper as your padding instead.

PRINTING AND EMBELLISHING TECHNIQUES

PRINTING OPTIONS

Many of the techniques you learned in the Paper chapter work for fabrics too. When printing on fabrics, the important things to remember are: Always wash, dry, and iron your fabric first. Washing removes any stiffening agents and preshrinks the fabric slightly, while ironing creates a smooth, flat surface for printing.

HAND-PRINTING

Several hand-printing methods were covered in the Paper chapter, but fabric has a few unique requirements. First, remember to prep the fabric as described on pages 68-69, and use fabric-friendly inks. The final result will depend on the type of fabric you use: Fine details print better on tightly woven cloth, but graphics printed on loose-weave fabrics have a natural, handmade feel. Once dry, cover your fabric with a lint-free cloth and heat-set it with an iron, according to the ink manufacturer's instructions.

HAND PAINTING

Hand painting your fabric with a brush or fabric marker is labor-intensive, and so is not suited to large-scale production. However, it's a great one-of-a-kind option for packaging luxury products or high-end pieces of art.

This page: Apple stamp by Gemma Behrens, Jac Whippet.
Opposite: Embroidered fabric tag by Urban Threads.

DIGITAL PRINTING

Digital printing (print-on-demand) for fabrics is one of the most exciting recent developments in the textile world because it allows for small-run printing (as little as 1 yard, or 90cm) at a reasonable price. This revolution opens up endless experimentation and customization opportunities for designer-makers. With some good prepping, you can even print fabrics on your home inkjet printer.

TRANSFERS

If your packaging artwork or logo contains many intricate details, consider transferring it onto your fabric instead of printing or painting it. Print the artwork onto iron-on transfer paper, place it face-down on the fabric, and iron. Voila! The image is instantly transferred. Another option is the image transfer method demonstrated on pages 32–33. It works just as well on fabric as it does on paper.

EMBROIDERY

Finally, embroidery is a great embellishing technique for fabrics because it creates a lovely texture and conveys a hand-crafted look and feel. Like hand-painting, this is a pretty labor-intensive technique, so it's more suited to small-scale production.

TIPS

Try working on a lightly padded surface, like an ironing board.

Wetting the fabric slightly before painting encourages colors to flow into each other, creating a beautiful watercolor effect.

SEE ALSO

Tutorial: *pp.68–69*
Digital printing sources in Resources: *p.170*

TUTORIALS

ROSE FABRIC WRAP

Wrapping with cloth is great because it's simple and requires few materials. But don't settle for just wrapping your product in fabric and calling it a day! This tutorial takes wrapping one step further by creating a knotted rose on top of the wrapped package.

BRAND
Joya Bindery

BRAND ATTRIBUTES
Joyful. Tailor-made. Inspired.

PRODUCTS
Handmade albums and books

PACKAGING NOTES
Joya Bindery creates custom, hand-bound books mostly for family albums and weddings. Floral motifs occur frequently in her designs, and since the majority of her clients are women, she wanted her packaging to be soft, feminine, and customized. Most of her books are ordered as gifts celebrating life's happy moments, so the packaging had to reflect a similarly joyous feel.

Materials used

- OBJECT TO BE WRAPPED (TWO BOOKS IN THIS CASE)
- 28 × 28 INCHES (71 × 71 CM) SQUARE FABRIC (LIGHTWEIGHT FABRICS SUCH AS COTTON, SILK, OR LINEN ARE ALL GOOD CHOICES)

1 Lay the fabric face down. Place books in the middle of it.

2 Take the side closest to you and tuck it under the books. Then take the opposite end and bring it over.

3 Gather one side and pull it toward the middle of the books. Repeat on the other side and tie a knot.

4 Pull one knot-end up and wrap the other around it. Tuck the end of the tip into itself. Now, repeat with the other knot-end.

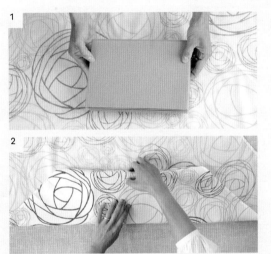

TIP
The bigger your wrap, the larger your rose will be! Tie the knot snugly so the corners are neat.

BLOCK PRINTING

In this tutorial, we will be tracing our artwork onto blocks of rubber and carving out the design to make our own custom printing blocks. The result is simple yet eye-catching and a wonderful way to enhance plain fabric packaging.

BRAND
Spark Baubles

BRAND ATTRIBUTES
Playful. Colorful. Striking.

PRODUCTS
Jewelry

PACKAGING NOTES
Spark Baubles designs and produces a jewelry line featuring fun shapes and vibrant colors. Generally their designs are geometric and have hard edges, so the owners wanted the packaging to have a soft touch (yet still hint at its contents). We thought it would be fun to package their pieces in handmade pouches with block-printed graphics reminiscent of their designs and colors.

Materials used

- FABRIC
- RUBBER CARVING BLOCK
- TRACING PAPER
- NO. 2 PENCIL
- BONE FOLDER OR SMALL SPOON
- LINOLEUM CUTTER WITH NO. 1 AND NO. 5 CUTTERS
- FABRIC INK PAD

1

I Print out a copy of the design you would like to use. Place a piece of tracing paper over it and start tracing the design. Turn the tracing paper face-down onto your carving block.

2

2 Transfer the image by rubbing the back of the paper with your bone folder or small spoon.

3

3 Carve the stamp from your block with your linoleum cutter. Use the No. 5 tip to carve away larger areas, and switch to No. 1 when you are working on the more intricate lines.

4 When you have finished, tap your stamp and blow off any remaining rubber crumbs. Take your ink pad and ink your stamp to make a test print, to check that there are no areas still to carve.

4

5 Once you're happy with the test results, you are ready to start stamping onto your fabric!

5

TIP
Keep the cutter at a 30° angle, and cut away from yourself. Don't forget—while the image will be reversed on the block, it will be right-side up when you stamp.

PRINTING ON FABRICS AT HOME

This tutorial explains the step-by-step process for printing on fabrics with your home printer. Yes, it can be done, so long as you are using an inkjet printer, not a laser printer. If your fabric needs to be washable, use the optional step in the tutorial.

BRAND
Coastarium

BRAND ATTRIBUTES
Limited edition. Natural. Eco-friendly.

PRODUCTS
Wooden coasters

PACKAGING NOTES
Coastarium creates coasters from reclaimed wood, and each one is hand-painted. No two coasters are identical, and the company wanted the packaging to reflect this uniqueness. Since the coasters will vary in size, we decided that using fabric to wrap each one would be our best choice. Each section of fabric can also be individually printed with various colors and graphics.

Materials used

- FABRIC (100% COTTON RECOMMENDED)
- FREEZER PAPER
- IRON
- CUTTING MAT
- UTILITY KNIFE WITH A SHARP BLADE
- INKJET PRINTER
- OPTIONAL: FABRIC RINSE AND SET SOLUTIONS (E.G., BUBBLE JET SET AND BUBBLE JET RINSE)

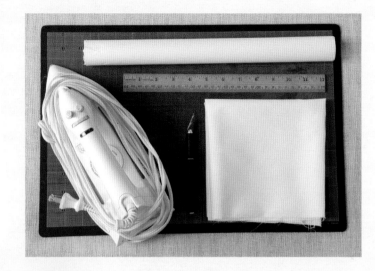

1. Prep your fabric by washing and ironing to make it easier to work with and to help the inks to absorb better and last longer. Optional step: At this point, if you want your fabric to be washable, set it with a rinse solution and follow the instructions on the product label.

2. Cut the fabric and freezer paper to a slightly bigger size than your printer can accommodate. (Usually 8½ × 11 inches/21.5 × 27.9 cm).

3. Place your freezer paper on top of your ironed fabric with the shiny side down. Run a medium-hot, dry iron over the freezer paper and it will adhere to your fabric.

4. Using your utility knife and ruler, trim the fabric and freezer paper to 8½ × 11 inches.

5. Feed the sheet through your printer, peel off the freezer paper backing, and voila, your very own printed fabric! It's now ready to be used to package your product. Optional step: Rinse and wash the fabric with cold water and fabric rinse to remove excess ink. Some fading may occur, depending on your preferred inks, but your fabric is now permanent and washable.

MATERIALS AND HOW TO USE THEM

—

ALTERNATIVE MATERIALS

Metals, ceramics, and glass are all reusable materials, a quality that makes them sustainable packaging solutions. Metal and glass can be recycled many times and are extremely durable, as are ceramics. Metals, ceramics, and glass can also be made food-safe, and they all protect against dirt and moisture.

TYPES OF ALTERNATIVE MATERIALS

When considering these materials for your packaging, be mindful that they can often be heavy, which will increase your shipping costs. Lightweight options could well be available, so be sure to do your research before settling on your material. And, you may need to factor in breakages if you're using a fragile material.

METALS
Metal packaging—typically aluminum, steel, or tin—is a popular option for bath and beauty products, and food items. Aluminum and steel containers are durable, keep foods sterilized longer, and are tamper-resistant. Recycled tin containers can be bought in bulk online, in specialty stores and from salvage and thrift outlets.

CERAMICS
Ceramics are usually made of clay and typically categorized as either earthenware, stoneware, or porcelain. Containers can be found in many craft supply stores and online, and can be embellished in several ways, for example using glazes and decals.

GLASS
The preserving qualities of glass make it an ideal option for liquid foods and perishables, as well as non-food products like plants and candles. Being transparent, glass showcases interesting shapes and colors well, while colored glass could also help distinguish products of different flavors and styles.

WOOD
Wood packaging has long been used for foods, wine, furniture and other large products because of its sturdiness. As packaging, the weight and color of the wood are also important factors.

Opposite: Mason jar by Nicole Ebbitt, The Caramel Jar.
This page: Containers made from ceramics, glass, and metal.

USES OF ALTERNATIVE MATERIALS

BOTTLES AND JARS

Bottles or jars are typically made of glass, ceramic, or metal, and are good options for food products such as honey or candy, as well as beauty and home products like balm, candles, or lotion. These materials lend a high-quality touch to the overall packaging and keep perishables fresh for a while. Consider size, weight, color, and any special features you may need (such as a wide rim, air-tightness, or food-safety).

PRE-PRINTED BOTTLES

If you need large quantities, consider pre-printing on stock bottles or jars from your printer. Alternatively, hand-print them yourself by stenciling, stamping, or applying decals (tutorial on pages 92–93). Bottled products tend to be reused over time, so keep in mind that you will need to heat-set your artwork to make it permanent. To keep things simple, you could have your product and brand information on a separate piece, such as a pre-printed hangtag that people can remove as needed. If you are selling food products, pre-wash the bottles and make sure they are food-safe.

This page: Silk screen labels on glass bottles by Aubrey Levitt, Body & Eden; design by Jennifer Schwartz.
Opposite left: Digitally printed kraft label by Stacey Humpherys, Girl*In*Gear Studio.
Opposite right: Screen printed porcelain candle by Frederick Bouchardy, Joya.

STORE-BOUGHT BOTTLES WITH ADHESIVE LABELS

Alternatively, you can purchase your bottles and jars in bulk from craft and packaging supply stores, or at your local flea market, and customize your product labels on the computer (tutorial on pages 48–49). Run them through your printer and resize them as needed to fit varying package sizes. This is an efficient and economical solution for products with multiple flavors and styles.

SPECIAL FEATURES

With the variety of metal, glass, and ceramic jars and bottles available, don't settle for a generic glass jar. Some glass bottles have interesting patterns, or perhaps your packaging calls for an opaque option like vintage milk glass? Explore different finishes on metals: matte or high-gloss and glazes on ceramics. Think about any special features required for your bottle packaging: Does your product need an air-tight lid? Does the bottle need to be food-safe? These are all factors worth thinking about as you consider your packaging options.

TIP

If you're using found or used bottles and jars, be sure to clean them thoroughly beforehand, especially if you are packaging edible products.

BOXES

Boxes are good packaging options for many types of products including foods and perishable products, beauty products, paper goods, and jewelry. They tend to be used for shipping smaller items. If bundling products, a metal or ceramic basket is an attractive way to package multiple items.

BOXES

Metal boxes are generally made of lightweight alloys like tin or aluminum. Boxes like this can be bought in bulk (see Resources, page 170) and can easily be pre-printed or hand-printed using techniques like stenciling and stamping, or applying transfers and labels. Glass and ceramic boxes are exquisite and tend to showcase precious objects well, such as jewelry and accessories. Wooden boxes can add a beautiful rustic feel to your presentation, along with having the advantage of protecting fragile items.

BOXES WITH ADHESIVE LABELS

With store-bought blanks, you can customize your product labels and run them through your printer (see tutorial on pages 48–49). This is an efficient and economical solution for product lines with multiple flavors or styles.

TIP

Compartmentalized boxes are especially useful for separating products with different flavors, such as teas, spices, and confections.

SHAPED BOXES

If the generic rectangular box is not for you, consider custom-made or found boxes that feature unique shapes or patterns. Just as important is its function. For example, a plant will need a box that allows light in, whereas you may need a heat-resistant box for candles. Some boxes are so beautiful by themselves they need no embellishment, except perhaps a hangtag or a card insert. If you sell one-of-a-kind items, perhaps each box will differ per customer to reflect the uniqueness of your product. Flea markets and antique shops are great places to find unique and interesting boxes.

WIRE AND CERAMIC BASKETS

When selling in sets or handling unwieldy items, the wire or ceramic basket is a good way of keeping everything together as a package, plus the basket can be reused. And don't forget to brand the basket with your company hangtag or insert!

Opposite: Recycled wooden box by Laura Johnson and Kirsten Elyse Nurge, Elysium Apothecary.
This page: Wire baskets can be a good way of keeping awkwardly shaped products together in one place.

TAGS AND LABELS

Tags and labels made from these materials are unique and can really catch people's attention. They have lots of practical advantages too: They're durable, often waterproof, and one-size-fits-all. Plus, you can use the same tag for all of your products (as long as the information is not product-specific), consequently saving on production costs.

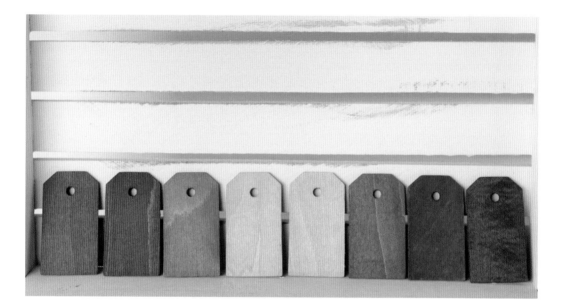

WOODEN TAGS

Wooden tags in their original form lend a natural touch to your packaging. They can easily be painted in a rainbow of colors. Text and images are easily applied by pre-printing, or embellished by stamping, screen printing, stenciling, or simply hand-lettering on them.

GLASS TAGS

Glass is seldom used for tags and labels due to its fragility, and printing on it can be costly. If this is not of concern, glass could well be the ideal material to help your brand stand out!

> **TIP**
> Specialty tags are ideal for high-end or custom items, such as jewelry, luxury candles and beauty products, or fashion accessories.

CERAMIC TAGS

Compared to metal, ceramic tags are far easier to embellish on your own. You might consider painting, hand-illustrating or stamping them (see tutorial on pages 82–83). Or, you might opt to buy ready-made tags and hand-write on them with markers. Other embellishment options include the addition of glitter, or even edge painting (painting on the edges of the tags) for an extra touch of sophistication. Or, you might consider custom shapes and sizes to make your tags more distinctive to your brand.

METAL TAGS

Metal hangtags can be bought in bulk and pre-printed with your brand information by engraving, stamping, or embossing. When selecting the metal, finish, size, and shape for your tags, consider how those factors best reflect your brand. If you choose to make the tags yourself, you'll need to invest in metal stamps and a hammer. Keep in mind that DIY is best suited to smaller quantities, because the process is pretty labor-intensive.

Opposite: Hand-stained wooden hangtags by Natalie Jost, Olive Manna.
This page: Clay gift tags with distressed acrylic paint finish by Michaela Houston, Mondän.

PRINTING AND EMBELLISHING TECHNIQUES

PRINTING OPTIONS

Some of the printing techniques we discussed in the previous chapters, such as screen printing and stenciling can be applied to metals, ceramics, and glass. There are some additional techniques you might try too, like etching metal or glass, burning wood (pyrography) or stamping ceramics. Be sure to test them first to ensure the method works the way you expect it to.

COMMERCIAL PRINTING

Industrial inkjet printing on metal, ceramics, and glass usually involves printing directly onto the surface with special inks and setting it with high heat. This method is wonderful if your artwork is extremely detailed or photographic in nature. Or, you can print onto special transfer paper, adhere it to the material, and transfer it to your packaging, also known as transfer printing. It is possible to create decals or transfers at home, but in order to make them adhere permanently to your surface, you will need heat-setting equipment such as a kiln or an oven.

HAND-PRINTING

Silk-screen printing onto these materials at home usually means using transfer paper, because of the properties of the surfaces, and because glass, ceramic, and metal containers may be too curved, angled, or awkwardly shaped to allow this. For the more adventurous, however, there are ways! You could try using pieces of ordinary foam from a craft or fabric store (about 2–3 inches/5.5–7.5 cm thick), and silk screen directly onto it. Then, carefully bend the foam around your curved/angled object so that it transfers the silk screen design onto it. The key is to use the right inks/glaze for your material.

PAINTING

Of course, hand-painting on glass, ceramic, and metal will give a lovely one-of-a-kind feel, but this is only really practical for quite small-scale packaging. There is a wide variety of special kinds of paint and ink for these surfaces readily available in art stores and online. You could, for example, create a beautiful faux stained-glass effect using transparent glass paints and fake leading (that comes in a tube); or, using enamel paints, create some striking designs on metal.

CUSTOM ADHESIVE LABELS

If the techniques mentioned above sound overwhelming or a bit too time-consuming, you might consider purchasing pre-made metal or glass containers and creating your own customized adhesive packaging labels. The tutorial on pages 48–49 includes downloadable templates that you can use to start designing your own labels.

STAMPING, STENCILING, AND ETCHING

Similarly, when applying hand-printing techniques to metal, glass, or ceramics, whether it be stenciling, stamping, or etching (see tutorials on pages 46–47, 80–81, and 82–83), be sure to use the right inks. When using trickier substances such as vitrifying inks, many designers opt to use professional printers to produce transfer labels since many of these inks require a high heat to adhere permanently.

Opposite: Metal churn with printed label by Pandora Bell; design by Studio Output.
This page: Glass bottles wrapped in washi tape by Beatriz Gaspar, Con Botas de Agua.

TUTORIALS

ETCHING ON GLASS

Etching on glass is not as challenging as it sounds. It's a great way to customize your glass packaging without spending a fortune. Initially, it will require some practice on your part, but, once you get the hang of it, the process is quick and the result is elegant.

BRAND
Starry Night Preserves

BRAND ATTRIBUTES
Fresh. Handcrafted. Unique and sophisticated blends and flavors.

PRODUCTS
Flavored jellies and preserves

PACKAGING NOTES
Starry Night Preserves produce fresh gourmet jellies and preserves in small batches. The owners wanted their packaging to showcase their unique variety of blends and flavors, and also highlight the handmade process. We felt that glass canning jars with some etching would be the way to go.

Materials used

- GLASS CANNING JARS
- CONTACT PAPER OR ADHESIVE PAPER
- CUTTING MAT
- UTILITY OR CRAFT KNIFE WITH A SHARP BLADE
- ETCHING CREAM (SUCH AS ARMOUR ETCH, AVAILABLE FROM CRAFT STORES)
- PROTECTIVE GLOVES
- BRUSH
- MARKER OR PEN

1. Draw or trace the artwork onto the contact paper.

2. Use your utility knife to cut out the artwork. This is your stencil.

3. Position your stencil and smooth it onto the glass jar completely, making sure there are no loose edges or bubbles.

4. Don't forget to wear your gloves for this step! Brush a generous amount of etching cream onto the area you'd like to etch. Refer to the instructions that come with your particular etching cream for information and drying time.

TIP
Any glass the cream touches will be altered, so you need to be careful and contain it just to the area you want etched.

BRANDED CLAY TAGS

Think beyond paper for your hangtags and make your own branded clay tags with polymer clay and custom rubber stamps. You can easily make them in batches to suit your needs, and they can really add a touch of sophistication to your packaging.

BRAND
Love, Poppy

BRAND ATTRIBUTES
Sophisticated. Minimalist.

PRODUCTS
Clothing and accessories

PACKAGING NOTES
Love, Poppy is a textile studio that creates handmade fashion accessories and clothing. Since all their goods have a soft tactile quality to them, we thought it would be a great idea to incorporate a contrasting element in their packaging: clay tags.

Materials used

- OVEN-BAKE POLYMER CLAY
- BAKING DISH (SEE YOUR SPECIFIC CLAY BRAND'S INSTRUCTIONS)
- A ROLLING PIN
- A TOOTHPICK
- A COOKIE CUTTER IN WHATEVER SHAPE YOU WANT
- RIBBONS OR TWINE
- RUBBER STAMPS OR CARVING TOOLS FOR CREATING ARTWORK
- AN OVEN
- A PAINT PEN (OPTIONAL)

1. Roll the polymer clay out into a thin, even sheet, about ⅝ inch thick (1.58 cm). Using your cookie cutter, cut out the tag shapes.

2. Poke the top of all your tags with your toothpick to make holes for stringing them.

3. Transfer your tags onto your baking sheet and stamp them lightly using your stamps. Bake the tags according to the instructions on your clay box.

4. Once they are baked and cooled, string ribbons through the tags. You can, if you wish, embellish them further with a paint pen.

TIP
For a bigger hole, use a straw or a skewer.

MATERIALS AND HOW TO USE THEM

REPURPOSED AND UPCYCLED MATERIALS

If one of the attributes of your brand is eco-friendliness, you might want to repurpose materials for your packaging. Repurposing is essentially using a product for an alternative purpose than it was originally intended for. In packaging, this could mean simply using recycled paper to create your branded hangtag, or using scrap wood to create a wooden box, or any number of other options. Upcycling takes it a step further: It means turning waste objects into new products of a superior function and also improved environmental value. Examples include taking a piece of used wire and turning it into a hanger, or making a handbag from scrap fabric.

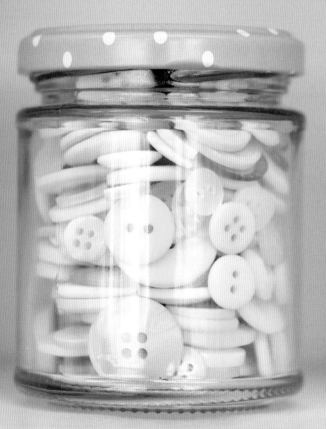

TYPES OF REPURPOSED MATERIALS

For the purposes of this chapter, we will delve into intact, found objects that you might use to house your product. We will also discuss repurposing materials to hold your product or augment its overall packaging.

PAPER
So many types of paper materials can be repurposed: paint samples, newspapers, old sewing patterns and maps, and cardboard, to name a few. To embellish, you can draw, print, stamp, stencil, or layer them to create new textures.

FABRICS
You can easily turn found fabrics into bags, pouches and wraps, or use them to embellish other types of packaging, such as a cloth hangtag. Consider embroidering or printing your brand logo on them. Cut them up or sew different scraps together for an interesting visual effect.

PLASTIC, GLASS, AND METAL
Used plastic, glass, and metal bottles and containers can be fashioned into packaging as long as they are in good condition, properly cleaned, and safe for reuse. If your products are for consumption, ensure the containers comply with food safety regulations. Print your brand identity directly on the containers or wrap them with printed papers and labels.

Opposite: Repurposed jars are great for packaging small items.
This page: Etched wooden block by Sarah Rainwater Designs; design by Sarah Rainwater and Sarah Verity.

WOOD

Wood has long been used to package goods and using recycled wood is an appealing to convey a sense of heritage for custom or unique items. Driftwood found on beaches can add a sense of rustic beauty and charm as well as providing material for one-off, unique pieces. Wood scraps can be further cut down to make smaller containers. There are many ways to embellish wood, such as hand-painting, stamping, stenciling, carving, pyrography (burning into the wood), and decals.

CORK

Cork is an extremely versatile material, as it's easy to cut into different sizes and shapes. It's also light and attractive, and can be reused multiple times. It is also fire-resistant. You can buy cork in sheets or rolls, which you can then cut to your needs, or in pre-cut shapes. The most common way to print on cork is silk-screen printing, but it is also possible to stencil, hand-draw, or carve on it.

This page: Hand-built and stamped raw pine boxes by PieBox.
Opposite: Repurposed atlas pages used as gift-wrap by Amber, Heather and Alyssa Overton, Joyful Creations.

UPCYCLING IDEAS

The idea behind upcycling is to offset the use of new raw materials, which in turn reduces energy usage and pollution. Here are a few ideas to get you started if you choose to experiment with it.

- Hollow out corks from wine bottles to house small items
- Cut out book pages to create wraps or boxes
- Use old maps, atlases, and recycled papers to create tags and wraps
- Repaint metal containers (or cover them in scrap fabric) and add functionality, such as handles
- Cut up old clothing to package/protect fragile products
- Crochet strips of old plastic bags into unique bags and pouches

USES OF REPURPOSED MATERIALS

BOXES, BAGS, AND BOTTLES

There are many found objects you can use for your packaging. However, sometimes, the beauty of found, repurposed or upcycled items is their aged or unembellished state. In fact, you may choose to incorporate the faded etching on your found glassware, or flourishes and lettering on old cigar boxes, instead of trying to hide these "flaws."

FOUND CONTAINERS

Whether paper, plastic, wooden, or metal, found boxes can be a charming option for your product. Think of used wooden crates, jewelry boxes, used paint cans, cigar boxes, old cardboard boxes, and even drawers. They're all blank canvases waiting to be embellished with your brand markings. If you are using the box in its found, unembellished state, completing the package with a branded hangtag or card insert is an understated but effective way to retain the company branding and assert its eco-friendly credentials. Chewing the Cud, my San Francisco-based design studio, creates a line of limited-edition gift presentation sets known as "Limitée." Each set is packaged in a found cigar box, with no two sets looking the same. Each Limitée box comes with a hand-sewn, numbered certificate of ownership for that extra high-end, exclusive touch.

This page: Decorating glass jars with fabric is a good way to make your packaging stand out.
Opposite top: Candles in repurposed wine bottles with letterpressed labels by Rewined; design by Stitch Design Co.
Opposite bottom: Repurposed egg carton with adhesive label by Dominique Gros, L'art de la Curiosité.

MODIFIED CONTAINERS

In some instances, you may find you only need a portion of the found box or container. For example, you might only use the bottom half of your found bottles to pour your handmade candles into, which you could enhance with a branded label and wax seal as a finishing touch. If you don't care for the object's found appearance, you might choose to spray paint, stencil, stamp, or apply transfers and labels to them.

REPURPOSED AND UPCYCLED BAGS AND WRAPS

Paper and cloth shopping bags can be printed on to create unique packaging options, or simply cut them up to make wraps. Found embellishments such as buttons, twine, or unusual strings and ribbons make good enclosures. Old sweaters and shirts can be cut up to create bags and pouches. Pillowcases are practically ready-made bags or covers for packaging. Embellish these fabrics by hand-stamping, stenciling, or embroidering.

CONTAINERS FROM WASTE MATERIAL

Don't discount what initially may look like "trash." Containers made from waste material can provide great backdrops for embellishing due to their natural tones. Think of berry boxes, egg cartons, and paper tubes, for example. It doesn't take much to spruce them up into attractive packaging solutions, from hand-printing (spray-painting, silk-screen printing, stenciling, block-printing) to applying transfers, decals, labels, and tags. These materials are often pretty sturdy and can double as protection and padding for the products.

FINISHING TOUCHES

In some cases, you might use recycled or upcycled materials as finishing touches for your packaging. Finishing touches could be wraps, ties, tags, labels, attachments, or enclosures.

WRAPS AND TIES

Wraps or ties made of found fabric or plastic scraps can be wonderful accents. The individuality of found pieces adds a unique touch to your packaging that is not easily replicated.

This page: Old sewing-pattern wrap, scrap-fabric ribbon and scrap-paper tag by Ashley Connelly, The Creative Place.
Opposite top: DVD pocket made from kraft butcher paper with scrap-paper tags by Nikki Mihalik, Akula Kreative.
Opposite bottom: Scrap felt DVD pocket with photo hangtag by Nikki Mihalik, Akula Kreative.

TAGS AND LABELS

Take a look around your home and workplace, and you will be sure to find materials that you can easily transform into tags and labels. These could be papers, paint chip samples, cardboard packaging, plastic sheets, scrap fabrics, wood, cork, and even pieces of metal. Layer thin papers together to create a tag, or paste fabric over cardboard packaging. Drill a hole on found pieces of wood, tie a piece of string, and hand-illustrate or rubber-stamp on them before attaching them to your product.

ATTACHMENTS AND ENCLOSURES

Don't discount seemingly mundane supplies, such as metal rings and wires. Many household and office supplies can be upcycled to make finishing touches for packaging products. For instance, safety pins make handy attachments for fabric products, especially when coupled with found strings, ribbons, or lace. All of these can be dyed to match your brand color, or hand-printed upon. Rubber bands and elastics, as well as wire ties, strings, used yarn, and rope all make good enclosures, with minimal cost. You can find buttons in thrift stores in a variety of shapes, sizes, and colors, and they make for unique and interesting enclosures.

TUTORIALS

MAKING YOUR OWN DECALS

This tutorial shows you how to make your own decals using image transfer paper. Image transfer is a great DIY technique for adhering graphics onto many surfaces and personalizing your packaging, particularly when used with repurposed materials.

BRAND
Mighty Candles

BRAND ATTRIBUTES
Imaginative. Eco-friendly.

PRODUCTS
Soy candles

PACKAGING NOTES
Mighty Candles invite customers to create their own experience when using their candles, and the company wanted to emphasize the uniqueness and ingenuity of their products. So, their candles are housed in found metal containers, and labeled with decals with a variety of designs.

Materials used

- INKJET DECAL PAPER
- INKJET PRINTER
- SCISSORS
- NEEDLE
- BRUSH
- SQUEEGEE
- BOWL OF WATER
- VARNISH (OIL-BASED IF YOU PREFER A TRANSPARENT DECAL)

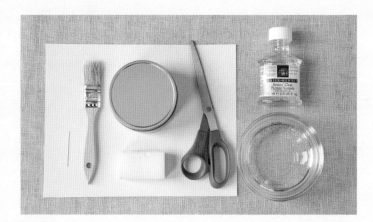

1 Using your inkjet printer, print your image onto the matte side of a sheet of inkjet decal paper. Dry for at least an hour. Cut out the decal, leaving a small border around the edges. If you prefer a transparent decal, coat it with an oil-based varnish. Allow the varnish to dry between applications.

2 Drop the decal into a bowl of water and soak it for a couple of minutes to help loosen the backing paper.

3 Use your paintbrush to apply varnish over the area where you want to stick your decal.

4 Remove the decal from the water. Slide the backing off and position the decal face-up on the tin. Use a squeegee to remove excess water and eliminate air bubbles.

5 For additional protection, use your paintbrush to coat the decal with varnish and allow it to dry.

TIP
Change your printer setting to "low-volume ink," because excess ink could run when you dip your decal into water.

DESIGNING YOUR PACKAGING

Picture a beautifully decorated cupcake, sitting temptingly on a hand-painted plate with a fork beside it, daring you to take the first bite. While it may seem like the cupcake is the main attraction, it's also the presentation on a beautiful plate with a fork and its fresh aroma that is really tempting you to break that diet! Impactful packaging is like that. Rarely is it one single element that beckons to us; usually it's the overall styling and presentation that captures our attention. In this section, we will look at different product categories and delve into the special considerations that will enhance your packaging style.

DESIGNING YOUR PACKAGING

JEWELRY, CERAMICS, AND GLASS

With fragile products, avoiding breakages is obviously a high priority. Over and above this, you need to be mindful of how you will be selling them—whether individually or in sets—and how they'll be transported. You'll also have to consider the environment in which the product will be sold—in brick-and-mortar stores, online, or through another outlet.

All these factors will influence which packaging materials you use, as well as the shape and size of the package. You also need to ensure that the cost of your packaging doesn't eat into your profit margin. For example, small items such as jewelry and ornaments look especially precious when presented in unique bags and containers, but this packaging may cost more. In this chapter, I'll present some interesting ideas for fragile items, as well as some special considerations.

FLINT by mine

Nº 55 cc •
100 percent soy wax hand
poured candle
custom blended & made to order
mine
CALIFORNIA

Previous page: Letterpress-printed tags and cards by Alischa Herrmann, Bespoke Letterpress.
This page: Flint candle with die-cut corrugated box and hand-stamped gift tag by Judith Parker, Mine Design.
Opposite: Badger brooches on hand-printed kraft tag with string tie by Elizabeth Pawle, Elizabeth Pawle Illustration.

PACKAGING MATTERS

The very nature of these products means there'll often be a pressing need to balance practical factors such as protecting expensive items with more aesthetic-driven considerations. How do you maintain the integrity of your brand packaging while ensuring its functionality?

WILL YOU BE SELLING YOUR ITEMS IN SETS?

If you're selling items in sets, slotted boxes or inserts within a bigger box can act as dividers. You can also opt to wrap the pieces individually and use different icons or graphics to indicate each one. However, if you're planning to place several breakable items in one box, be sure they don't touch each other.

This reduces the chances of the products knocking against each other and getting chipped or broken. If you have a product that can be sold individually instead, you might want to opt for simpler, more versatile packaging so that your brand identity isn't lost.

DO THE PRODUCTS NEED TO BE TRANSPORTED?

If you are selling your ceramics and glass pieces at fairs and events, your customer will need a safe way to bring them home. Be sure to include plenty of padding to avoid breakage.

With face-to-face customer sales, boxes, bags, and wraps are all feasible solutions for individual breakable pieces such as pottery or glass. On the other hand, if you are shipping the order, be sure to layer the piece with protective papers or bubble wrap before packing it up.

Ceramics and glassware also benefit from padding materials like shreddded brown paper, as it can be squished tightly around the item, ensuring every part is well cushioned and protected.

Opposite: Card backing to hold brooches by Verónica de Arriba, Depeapa.
This page: Ceramic mug in a gift box with porcelain seal by Jude Winnall, VanillaKiln.

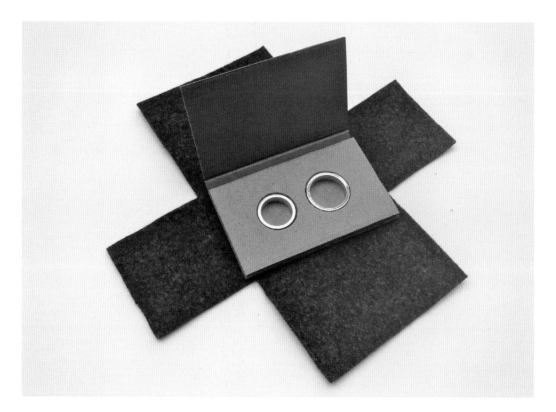

ARE YOUR PRODUCTS SMALL AND VALUABLE?

Mini pouches, bags, and envelopes are lovely ways to present jewelry and other small items. There are so many different approaches and techniques. Fastening options include drawstrings, ribbon ties, eye-hooks, buttons, and press fasteners. You can sew in a traditional method that hides the seam, or you can use the stitching as part of the external design, with maybe even a serrated edge using special scissors. As for embellishing, you can hand-print, appliqué, stamp, sew on some distinctive braiding or tassels, or use fabric markers to hand-draw a design.

Small boxes come in a variety of shapes and styles for an exquisite presentation. They also serve the purpose of protecting against moisture and damage. You don't have to limit yourself to generic cardboard or leather jewelry boxes though; you can always customize them with hand-printing or painting. Better yet, you might consider designing your own

box, or using found containers, such as glass jars, vials, canisters, or wooden containers, or making your own boxes.

If you prefer to package your jewelry flat, how about securing them to some cards? The cards can double as your business cards, or as gift cards that can be personalized by the customer. Securing jewelry items such as necklaces and bracelets in this way also helps prevent them from becoming tangled and is an effective way of displaying the piece. Be careful to tape down delicate linked chains and beaded jewelry, as these can easily break when customers try to untangle them.

WHAT PRODUCT INFORMATION NEEDS TO BE INCLUDED IN THE PACKAGING?

This could include care, cleaning, and handling instructions, such as how to clean precious metal or specific storage guidance (e.g., store away from direct sunlight). You could also highlight any special features of the product.

Opposite: Wedding band box made from recycled card and felt by Karola Torkos, Karola Torkos Jewellery.
This page: Computer-printed kraft cardstock earring backer by Kat Miller, Cardinal House.

designer spotlight
RAE DUNN

Since discovering clay in 1993, Rae Dunn has been creating her line of ceramic art and selling it worldwide. Just as each piece has been built entirely by hand, her packaging is also treated with the same level of love and care. Her graphic design background and experience in the fashion industry have invaluably informed her packaging aesthetic.

Q & A

WHAT KIND OF ITEMS DO YOU CREATE?
Ceramic items such as dishware, plates, bowls, cups, vases, plaques, and salt-and-pepper sets.

WHERE DO YOU SELL YOUR GOODS?
I sell online (via Etsy) and at exhibitions, craft fairs, and other events.

HOW ARE THEY PACKAGED WHEN SOLD?
I wrap the item in bubble wrap, wrap that in corrugated cardboard, add a decorative paper, and then tie the package with a ribbon.

WHY DID YOU DECIDE TO PACKAGE THEM IN THIS WAY?
Because ceramics are so fragile, double wrapping with bubble wrap and cardboard adds extra strength and protection. I add the decorative Chinese paper as a nod to my heritage.

WHY DID YOU CHOOSE CARDBOARD?
I like the natural look and feel of the cardboard as the top wrap. While bubble wrap is essential for protection, it's nice that it isn't the first thing you see.

WHAT DO YOU THINK MAKES FOR IMPACTFUL PACKAGING WHEN SELLING TO A CUSTOMER?
I like that the final presentation looks like a present. My customers are always saying what a treat it is to open it up.

ARE THERE ANY ECO-FRIENDLY ELEMENTS TO YOUR PACKAGING?
The cardboard and paper are recyclable. The ribbon can be reused.

WHAT SPECIAL CONSIDERATIONS ARE THERE FOR SHIPPING CERAMICS?
Because of the fragility, items have to be very well wrapped. Multiple pieces packaged together must not touch each other or be stacked in the box.

Opposite: Corrugated cardboard packaging with decorative paper and ribbon.
This page left: Ceramic art dish.
This page right: Set of four ceramic bowls.

{ Rae has added the stamp of Wilma the dog (her sidekick) on the product tag for a lovely personal touch. }

designer spotlight
ROCK CAKES JEWELRY

After completing her jewelry degree and working in fine jewelry production for eight years, Sarah Meredith set up her own brand, Rock Cakes. Taking her inspiration from everyday life, she never leaves home without her sketchbook and camera, as an idea can pop up at any moment.

Q & A

WHAT KIND OF ITEMS DO YOU CREATE?
People have said my work is a mix of beautiful, quirky, and cute. I aim to make jewelry that you'll want to treasure forever—jewelry to fall in love with.

WHERE DO YOU SELL YOUR GOODS?
I'm a massive fan of online retail, particularly Etsy, as it fits in well with taking care of my daughter. I also sell at craft fairs and in a few UK stores.

HOW ARE THEY PACKAGED WHEN SOLD?
My high-end items are boxed, the more expensive pieces in leather boxes, embossed with "Rock Cakes" and a tiny bird. My less expensive pieces come in kraft card boxes hand-stamped with specially ordered stamps. All items have handmade tags with black ribbon.

WHY DID YOU DECIDE TO PACKAGE THEM IN THIS WAY?
Most of my packaging was not a conscious decision, but the one thing I thought through was my tags. Standard jewelry tags are pretty ugly and I wanted them to be super pretty.

WHAT ARE SOME OF THE CHALLENGES YOU'VE FACED WITH PACKAGING?
Huge increases in postal costs have forced me to reduce the package sizes. Now the outer postal box is the packaging, my item inside is tissue wrapped, and I print little stickers and tie them with ribbon.

WHAT DO YOU THINK MAKES FOR IMPACTFUL PACKAGING WHEN SELLING TO A CUSTOMER?
I think it's often the make-or-break aspect of getting a repeat customer. It's about that feeling of euphoria when you open something special; it can get people hooked to your brand.

ARE THERE ANY ECO-FRIENDLY ELEMENTS TO YOUR PACKAGING?
I use a method called Gocco to print Rock Cakes postcards on repurposed cardboard boxes. I use a design on the front with the postcard print on the reverse. Gocco printing can be expensive, but this recycling saves money and helps the environment.

WHAT SPECIAL CONSIDERATIONS ARE THERE FOR SHIPPING JEWELRY?
I need my packages to arrive safely and undamaged, so I like to use boxes rather than padded envelopes to keep them secure. Besides, I think receiving a little box is more exciting.

Opposite: Hand-stamped kraft box.
This page: Postcards.

DESIGNING YOUR PACKAGING

FOODS AND PLANTS

Creating an impactful presentation for edible items can often be a challenge because there are so many other factors, such as shape, number of servings, and expiration dates to consider. In some cases, the primary packaging (which holds the food) has to meet additional requirements such as protecting the food item from elements like moisture, sunlight, or even chemicals. These extra considerations can play a deciding role in how you pacakage perishable items such as food and plants. In this chapter I'll discuss packaging considerations for all kinds of products, from cupcakes and other sweets to preserves, and from herbs and spices to plants.

PANDORA BELL
IRELAND
Handmade Lollipop
Made with Natural
Colours and Flavours
www.pandorabell.ie

PANDORA BELL
IRELAND
Handmade Lollipop
Made with Natural
Colours and Flavours
www.pandorabell.ie

This page: Die-cut adhesive sticker by Pandora Bell; design by Studio Output.
Opposite: Hand-built and stamped raw pine boxes by PieBox.

PACKAGING MATTERS

Packaging perishable items can be tricky as they are often fragile, uniquely shaped, or have a limited shelf life. Food products must also adhere to safety regulations.

WILL THERE BE MULTIPLE SIZES, FLAVORS, OR SHAPES?

Compartmentalized boxes or cupcake inserts can act as dividers for flavors and colors. They also secure the item and minimize smearing. Cupcake liners act as separators for a variety box containing different types of sweets or cookies. Or, you can wrap each piece individually and use different icons or graphics to indicate flavors. When your items include multiple shapes and colors, a clear acrylic organizer with compartments is a delightful way to show them all off.

WILL YOU BE SELLING IN SINGLE SERVINGS OR BY THE BOX?

Individually wrapped candy or cookies in translucent cellophane bags are especially attractive when the food has interesting textures and colors. The bags can be color-coded or have stickers as enclosures to indicate flavor. You might also choose to wrap your candy in wax paper and hand-stamp your brand on the wrapper.

This page: Candy box with cupcake inserts by Jessica Wilcox, Modern Moments Designs.
Opposite top: Terrarium box with geometric lid by Amanda Guarini, A Guarini Design.
Opposite bottom: Pre-printed cellophane wrapper by Springhill Pantry; design by Swear Words.

CAN THE UNIQUE SHAPE OF YOUR PRODUCT BECOME PART OF THE PACKAGE?

If your product has a unique shape or size, what better way to showcase that than to incorporate it into the packaging itself. For instance, in this image, the shape of the terrarium becomes part of the lid.

WILL YOUR PRODUCT HAVE TOPPINGS?

Some confections, like cookies and chocolate for example, have delicate toppings. A box with fillers like tissue paper, can secure each item and its topping. Where icing is involved, your item will require some head room, in which case, you might need individual boxes.

[PENTAGONAL TEARDROP TERRARIUM]

Springhill Pantry.

APRICOT APPLE & HAZELNUT

SHARING SLICE

350G

WHAT PRODUCT INFORMATION NEEDS TO BE INCLUDED IN THE PACKAGING?

These might include ingredients, flavors, or the expiration date, for example. Such information could be presented directly on the primary packaging or on additional elements such as tags, labels, bellybands, or ribbons. For instance, handwritten tags tied with ribbons on jam jars offer a quick way to distinguish flavors or varieties. Perhaps wrap your cookies in a hand-printed cotton cloth for the homespun look, and add a note on the tag, thanking the customer for their purchase.

WHAT IF THE INFORMATION VARIES FOR EACH FLAVOR BUT YOU'RE WORKING WITH A LIMITED BUDGET?

Pre-printed stickers and tags are attractive, yet economical, approaches for communicating numerous product ingredients and flavors.

ARE YOU USING BASIC PAPERS FOR YOUR PACKAGING BUT NEED A FINISHING TOUCH FOR THAT "WOW" FACTOR?

Utilitarian papers such as wax, parchment, butcher, and kraft are all versatile options for wrapping food products. Pair that with a ribbon and a wax seal (see Resources, page 170) or an embossed graphic for a simple but elegant package. Hand-stamping, stenciling, hand-drawing, and screen printing are all fun ways of bringing a personalized touch to the packaging.

This page top: Divine Dairy wax cheese wrap; design by Frank Aloi Design Co.
This page left: Caramels in a brown wax bag and pre-printed label by Nicole Ebbitt, The Caramel Jar.
Opposite top: Heirloom seed kit design by Sarah Rainwater and Sarah Verity, Sarah Rainwater Design.
Opposite bottom: Homemade cookies in a jar with a wooden tag by Amy Kelly, That Winsome Girl.

WILL YOUR PRODUCT EXPIRE QUICKLY?

If you are working with perishables, you will probably need to highlight your expiration date, or find a way to package it to extend its shelf life. This varies greatly across products. For instance, coffee might need to be sealed in air-tight containers or bags, but herbs might need to "breathe." In the latter case, micro-perforated bags might be the way to go. It's best to do your research and test your options for a period of time before committing to your packaging solution. Furthermore, most food and perishable products are governed by labeling rules for safety reasons, so always make sure your packaging is compliant.

DO YOUR PRODUCTS HAVE UNIQUE SHAPES AND COLORS?

Transparent containers offer a great way to showcase your products. For example, a clear glass jar can show off details like the scalloped edges of the cookies in the image (right). Perhaps the shape of your package or tag could mimic the product shape, or a photographic image of the product could be incorporated into the packaging. Brand stickers can also be printed in various colors to easily distinguish the flavors or product types.

designer spotlight
BIRD AND FEATHER

Living in Los Angeles, Marianne Gardner and Sean Maginity were naturally surrounded by exquisite design, gorgeous plant life, and an entrepreneurial spirit. One thing led to another, and all three soon became an obsession. From this passion, Bird and Feather was born.

Q&A

WHAT KIND OF ITEMS DO YOU CREATE?

We create special items that bring plant life into homes, so we've got a line of planters designed for air plants, plus we sell terrariums and terrarium-making supplies.

WHERE DO YOU SELL YOUR GOODS?

We sell on our own website, wholesale to boutiques, and at craft fairs.

HOW ARE THEY PACKAGED WHEN SOLD?

For our air plant pots, we chose recycled kraft boxes stamped with our logo in black ink. We use crinkle-cut recycled kraft paper as bedding / protection. The finishing touch is an air plant care sheet, also printed in black ink on recycled kraft paper.

WHY DID YOU DECIDE TO PACKAGE THEM IN THIS WAY?

We wanted the design to be clean, the materials to be eco-friendly, and the cost to be low. For us, recycled kraft was the obvious choice. It's accessible, affordable, and we like the natural look.

DID YOU CONSIDER USING OTHER PACKAGING MATERIALS?

We zeroed in pretty quickly on what we wanted. We never even considered anything plastic or anything that wouldn't biodegrade.

WHAT DO YOU THINK MAKES FOR IMPACTFUL PACKAGING WHEN SELLING TO A CUSTOMER?

Simplicity, and a back-to-basics packaging approach—subtle, simple, timeless accents on utilitarian forms that suggest quality and taste.

ARE THERE ANY ECO-FRIENDLY ELEMENTS TO YOUR PACKAGING?

Almost everything we use for packaging is biodegradable. We always choose recycled paper products, and the see-through bags for our terrarium filler line are compostable.

WHAT SPECIAL CONSIDERATIONS ARE THERE FOR SHIPPING YOUR GOODS?

Live plants! But that primarily impacts our shipping speed—everything ships via UPS Priority.

{ Note that the logo placement (near the corner) takes into consideration that the giver might want to tie a ribbon around the box. }

Opposite: Kraft boxes with kraft crinkle paper padding.
This page left: Stamped kraft boxes with twine.
This page right: Stamped canvas bags.

designer spotlight
COME COMER

After having their second baby, Yuzo and Yoko Tamaki realized how tough it is for a new mom to juggle cooking, cleaning, and childcare. From this Come Comer was born: a catering service delivering healthy Japanese-style foods for moms and their families.

Q & A

WHAT KIND OF ITEMS DO YOU CREATE?
We provide healthy foods using locally sourced produce, cooked using traditional Japanese seasonings (real sake, soy sauce, mirin, etc.).

WHERE DO YOU SELL YOUR GOODS?
We sell at local events, like art festivals and organic markets. We also teach workshops and sell our products there.

HOW ARE THEY PACKAGED WHEN SOLD?
We use Furoshiki (Japanese-style fabric wraps) to deliver the food packages for Come Comer. Each package is accompanied by a chopstick-style tag and an insert with eating and storing instructions. For our Emperor Jams product line, we package them with Japanese washi paper using a traditional origami folding method.

WHY DID YOU DECIDE TO PACKAGE THEM IN THIS WAY?
We cherish our traditions and love the concept: minimal, reusable, and beautiful.

DID YOU CONSIDER USING OTHER PACKAGING MATERIALS?
We first looked at paper boxes for budgetary and printing reasons. However, we knew the box would likely be trashed after use. Undoubtedly, Furoshiki wrap is more expensive but it is reusable. Also, by using this method of packaging, we convey a sense of hospitality and originality.

WHAT DO YOU THINK MAKES FOR IMPACTFUL PACKAGING WHEN SELLING TO A CUSTOMER?
We chose vibrantly colored Furoshiki wraps to bring some cheer into busy moms' lives. Our Come Comer logo depicts our wraps being pulled on a wagon, and the brand name combines the Japanese word for rice, *come*, and the Spanish verb *comer* meaning to eat: So you are invited to "Eat rice!" Our Emperor Jams logo uses the iconic view of Mt. Fuji as seen from Hayama, our hometown, a tribute to our roots.

ARE THERE ANY ECO-FRIENDLY ELEMENTS TO YOUR PACKAGING?
Yes, Furoshiki is eco-friendly packaging, as you can reuse the wrapping in many ways.

> Using Furoshiki wrapping is a great way to add value to packaging as the recipient can use it again and again themselves.

Opposite: Fabric wrap with paper label.
This page left: Washi paper jam jar wrap.
This page right: Emperor jams and washi paper wrapping.

115

DESIGNING YOUR PACKAGING

BATH AND BEAUTY

More often than not, I have bought a candle or soap, not because I needed it, but because it was packaged so well that I had to have it. The presentation of the package was so compelling that it transcended the product itself. As the category suggests, these products are about celebrating beauty and enriching personal health, so it is important that their packaging reflects that experience. Many products in this category are sold as gifts, so going the extra mile to create a beautiful presentation will pay off. Due to the delicate nature of bath and beauty products, and their unique shapes and forms, it is important to consider specific factors, such as the need for a temperature-controlled environment, fragility, or a limited shelf life. Some of the products I'll discuss here are soaps, lotions, oils, and candles.

CURE

CURE YOUR BODY
CURE THE WORLD
ORANGE PEEL
DEAD SEA SALT SCRUB

CURE

CURE YOUR BODY
CURE THE WORLD
LIME GINGER
DEAD SEA SALT SCRUB

This page: Cheery colors and clean typography convey the rejuvenating qualities of Cure products.
Opposite: Chalkboard candle by Judith Parker, Mine Design.

PACKAGING MATTERS

This is a category where the visual impression of the packaging has a tremendous impact on the perceived value of the product. But it can't be all style over substance! Let's examine some of the practical issues of packaging bath and beauty items.

WILL THERE BE MULTIPLE FRAGRANCES, SHAPES, OR SIZES? DO THESE FACTORS NEED TO BE INDICATED AND, IF SO, HOW?

For products of the same type that are being sold as a set, a box with compartments could work nicely. If your product is uncolored and generic-looking (maybe to avoid using chemical dyes) but comes in a range of scents, wrapping them individually in different colored papers or bands is an attractive way of distinguishing the varieties. Alternatively, you might consider adding a color-coded tag or label for each one.

This page: Used wine bottles with letterpress-printed labels by Janet Coffman, Circle 21 Candles.
Opposite: Shave set packaged using a recycled craft box tied with lace, a glass bottle with tag, and a printed and hand-stamped soap label by Jen O'Connor, The Little Ragamuffin.

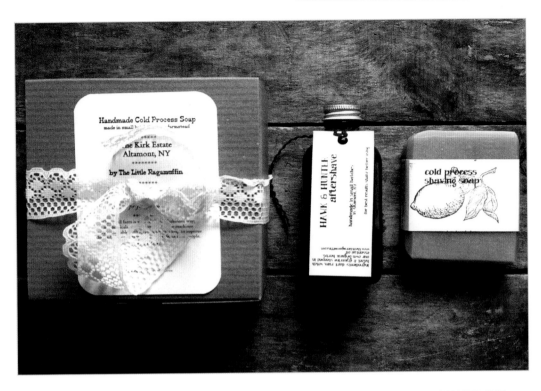

DO THE PRODUCTS NEED TO BE MOISTURE-, TEMPERATURE-, AND TAMPER-RESISTANT.

The integrity of beauty product packaging is usually paramount. Balms, creams, and lotions, especially those made with all-natural ingredients, have a short shelf life. Packaging them in appropriate containers, like tin canisters or dark plastic bottles to protect them from light and heat, will help to maximize their shelf life. A lot of crafters will pack lotions in smaller portions so the ingredients are still fresh at the end of usage. Furthermore, a squeeze bottle is better for unstable products like lotions than a tin or shallow container, because such products go bad more quickly when someone is putting their hands into them repeatedly. And finally, containers with tamper-resistant adhesive labels reassure customers of the products' purity.

MANY BATH AND BEAUTY PRODUCTS ARE SOLD AS GIFT SETS, CONTAINING ITEMS OF DIFFERENT SIZES AND SHAPES. HOW CAN THESE ITEMS BE PACKAGED TOGETHER?

In cases where your gift set contains a variety of product types, like balms, lotions, and soaps, you might utilize the same brand identity across all components and house the entire set in a branded box, bag, or basket. Not only does this cohesiveness create a more powerful presentation; if the different products are given away separately, your brand still appears on each component.

WITH SO MANY OF THESE PRODUCTS BEING SOLD AS GIFTS, HOW CAN THEY BE PERSONALIZED?

Consider using inserts, blank tags, and stickers to allow your customer to personalize the products after purchase. Adding a writeable finish to your container (such as chalkboard or dry-erase paint) is also a fun way to allow for personalization.

DO YOUR PRODUCTS REQUIRE INFORMATION LABELS?

There are standards and regulations for product information and warnings that vary depending upon your location. Be sure to confirm product regulations in your region before finalizing your packaging.

ARE YOUR PRODUCTS FRAGILE?

An important consideration is the fragility of beauty products, many of which are packaged in glass containers. Candle wax can crack if it isn't packaged properly, and containers might break or leak during transportation. Consider your sales channel(s): Do you sell directly to the customer? If so, packaging your lotion in a bottle and slipping it into a bag is sufficient, whereas if you are shipping in bulk to retailers, then you'll probably have to include padding and extra outer packaging.

This page top left and top right: Packaging for Hudson Made soaps incorporates offset printing, letterpress, and rubber stamping; design by Hovard Design.
This page main image above: Hand-stamped shipping labels by by Natalie Jost, Olive Manna.
Opposite: Soy candles in reusable glass jelly jars with kraft paper labels by Rachel Mueller, Oil & Wax.

HAND-PRINTING IS TOO LABOR-INTENSIVE AND PRE-PRINTING COMMERCIALLY IS OUT OF MY BUDGET. ARE THERE OTHER WAYS OF DIFFERENTIATING MY PACKAGING?

Understandably, it isn't always practical to hand-print every candle jar or lotion bottle, especially if you're fulfilling high-volume orders. Consider using textured or patterned glassware, or spray-painting a generic bottle with your brand color, then add to your packaging with a product label, tag, or insert.

IF YOUR PRODUCT IS HANDMADE AND 100 PERCENT ECO-FRIENDLY, HOW DO YOU CONVEY THAT WITH YOUR PACKAGING?

Going with reused or recycled materials is a wonderful way of communicating your brand message. There are other ways to reduce waste, though. You might initiate a jar return policy for a partial refund, for example, or encourage customers to reuse the packaging for other purposes.

designer spotlight
PRUNELLA SOAP

Janell Anderson started making soap in the summer of 2010 and taught herself the process by reading many books on soap-making history and traditional techniques. She works from her studio in Portland and sells her products in the United States and Canada.

Q & A

WHAT KIND OF ITEMS DO YOU CREATE?
I make soap using the old-fashioned cold-process method, with only plant-based ingredients, mostly food-grade herbs and spices, and essential oils.

WHERE DO YOU SELL YOUR GOODS?
I sell on Etsy and in a few boutiques around the United States and Canada.

HOW ARE THEY PACKAGED WHEN SOLD?
I print everything in-house and use patterned washi tape to differentiate the scents of the wrapped bars. Then, I tie the ends with natural hemp twine. I also make travel soap sticks that are packaged in natural cotton muslin bags and accented with kraft paper tags and labels.

WHY DID YOU DECIDE TO PACKAGE THEM IN THIS WAY?
My main goal was to use materials that could be easily recycled—no plastic packaging. It was also important to be able to use the same size labels across multiple product lines. I kept the printing process simple by only using black ink.

DID YOU CONSIDER USING OTHER PACKAGING MATERIALS?
I have been looking at other options, specifically moving to custom-printed boxes. The pros would be that others could do the packaging for me (currently, I tie all the wrapping myself). The drawback, of course, would be the cost!

WHAT DO YOU THINK MAKES FOR IMPACTFUL PACKAGING WHEN SELLING TO A CUSTOMER?
I am drawn to packaging that utilizes simple fonts and color palettes—keeping the packaging as simple and cost-effective as possible is key.

ARE THERE ANY ECO-FRIENDLY ELEMENTS TO YOUR PACKAGING?
Yes, all of the packaging materials are paper or fabric and are fully recyclable. I also use fully compostable cellophane bags.

WHAT SPECIAL CONSIDERATIONS ARE THERE FOR SHIPPING YOUR GOODS?
I use shredded kraft paper crinkles as packing material and only recycled kraft padded envelopes to ship the soap.

{ The patterned washi tape created a big splash for Prunella and charmed many (myself included) when they first saw it. }

Opposite: Individually wrapped and labeled soaps.
This page: Dog soap with kraft paper belly band.

designer spotlight

CIRCLE 21 CANDLES

Janet Coffman was inspired to create her own line of candles after visiting a candle company which used recycled wine bottles for its products. Being sensitive to smells, she disliked most of the scents available at the time. Determination, hard work, and a leap of faith, led to the inception of Circle 21 Candles.

Q & A

WHAT KIND OF ITEMS DO YOU CREATE?
We make premium soy candles, poured into used wine bottles that have been cleaned, cut, and sanded by hand. We use an all-cotton wick and high-end fragrance oils.

WHERE DO YOU SELL YOUR GOODS?
We are a wholesale business, but we have done limited consignments as well.

HOW ARE THEY PACKAGED WHEN SOLD?
We use letterpress-printed labels, on which the candle names are hand-stamped and color coordinated. Stamping is cost-effective and lends a handmade feel. The corks are also branded with our logo. We ship them in white cardboard boxes stamped with our logo and the scent name.

WHY DID YOU DECIDE TO PACKAGE THEM IN THIS WAY?
We looked at many packaging ideas, but the ones I liked the best were the most simple. That is Circle 21's ethos: K.I.S.S. (Keep It Simple, Stupid).

DID YOU CONSIDER USING OTHER PACKAGING MATERIALS?
The design firm I hired gets most of the credit for the great packaging. I gave a little direction: Something simple and classy, but on a tight budget.

WHAT DO YOU THINK MAKES FOR IMPACTFUL PACKAGING WHEN SELLING TO A CUSTOMER?
I think our brand simplicity makes it appealing. People like that we use a sustainable product like soy and are recycling used wine bottles.

ARE THERE ANY ECO-FRIENDLY ELEMENTS TO YOUR PACKAGING?
We are reusing wine bottles that would otherwise be trash.

WHAT SPECIAL CONSIDERATIONS ARE THERE FOR SHIPPING YOUR GOODS?
Candles are heavy and breakable. We have learned they travel well in their own cardboard box with some crinkle paper as filler. The individual boxes are then placed in bigger boxes with more filler (bubble wrap, peanuts, air bags, or paper) and lots of "FRAGILE" stickers!

Opposite: Used wine bottles with letterpress-printed labels.
This page: Branded cork lid.

DESIGNING YOUR PACKAGING

CLOTHES, SHOES, AND ACCESSORIES

Beyond white shirt boxes and paper bags, there are many ways to get creative when it comes to packaging your fashion products. In considering your options, be mindful of where and how your product will be displayed and shipped. In a store, customers will probably want to feel the product, or even open the packaging. Do your products have delicate trimmings that need to be packaged with care? Do your products wrinkle easily? How do you showcase and differentiate between styles and sizes?

This page: Printed fabric drawstring bag by Soma Intimates; design by Hovard Design.
Opposite: Inkjet-printed kraft bellyband by Christopher MacManus, Bittle & Burley.

BITTLE & BURLEY

HANDKERCHIEF

Made in Brooklyn

BITTLE & BURLEY

HANDKERCHIEF

Made in Brooklyn

PACKAGING MATTERS

This is often a tricky combination to get right, especially since many fashion products need to be opened, handled, and even tried on before purchase. Here we look at some of the functional issues and concerns for packaging clothes, shoes, and accessories.

WHAT TYPES OF PACKAGING WORK WELL FOR FASHION ITEMS?

If your clothing items call for an outside-the-box packaging format, consider using bags, tin cans, uniquely shaped cartons, or even tubes. T-shirts in tin cans are eye-catching and fun, and they're functional as the retailer can stack them for neat merchandizing. Stackability is also handy if you're shipping your product in large quantities. Shoes in bags instead of the traditional shoe box are a great way to convey that they're handmade or bespoke.

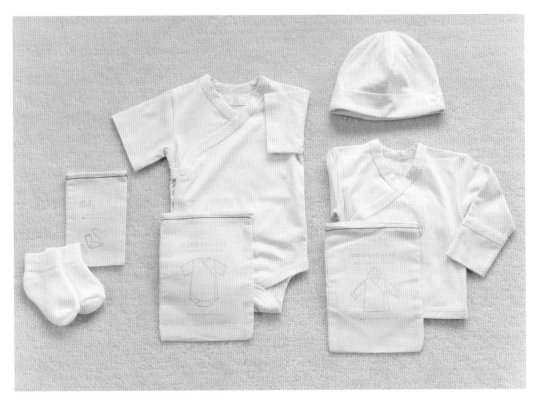

WHAT ARE SOME GREEN OPTIONS FOR PACKAGING YOUR FASHION ACCESSORIES?

There are many eco-friendly packaging options suitable for this category, especially since most of the products are foldable. For instance, scarves can be rolled up and fitted into repurposed berry boxes or egg cartons. Belts, clothing, and scarves all fit nicely into cardboard tubes. Not to mention, all of these containers are easy to embellish: Hand-stamping, stenciling, painting, illustrating, and block printing all work great for reclaimed packaging.

HOW DO YOU MAKE A SIMPLE BROWN BOX UNIQUE TO YOUR FASHION BRAND?

There is something totally classic about a brown box, and with a little creativity, you can definitely make it unique to your brand. Hand-stamping, stenciling, screen printing, and block printing are all great ways of embellishing your box without hurting your pocket. Think of your brand attributes and consider how the box can reflect them: Is your product whimsical? Elegant? Rustic? Perhaps a beautiful hand-dyed ribbon in your brand colors is a nice finishing touch. Maybe it's a witty message that makes your product's package memorable.

Opposite: Cotton shoe bags by Natalie Jost, Olive Manna.
This page: Stamped cotton bags for baby items by Yumiko Sekine, Fog Linen Work.

DOES YOUR PRODUCT NEED TO KEEP ITS SHAPE?

Some products, such as hats and bags, need to keep their shape. This is where I would recommend using a specialized box, like a hat box for example, to prevent damage. However, instead of settling for a generic box, try painting it in your brand colors, or marking it with your brand identity by stamping, stenciling, screen printing, or labeling it.

IS IT IMPORTANT FOR THE CUSTOMER TO EASILY VIEW COLORS OR STYLES WITHOUT OPENING THE PACKAGE?

If color and style are major draws for the product, consider a transparent packaging solution, such as plastic or glass. How about a resealable plastic box or a canning jar? A vellum bag paired with a branded adhesive label is a simple yet elegant solution too. Alternatively, bellybands and ribbons expose most of the product but help to keep things neat.

ARE YOUR PRODUCTS DELICATE?

Many fashion products are delicate, as they might have embellishments such as sequins, lace, or special add-ons like metal zippers and buckles, which are easily scratched. Be sure to cover the pieces with tissue before placing the product in its packaging. The tissue could be pre-printed with your logo to enhance the overall branding. Mesh bags are a viable option for delicate pieces, and can be easily hand-printed with your artwork.

This page: Fabric bags by Amie Nilsson, Merino Kids.
Opposite: Tote bags with translucent paper bellybands by Verónica de Arriba, Depeapa.

IS IT IMPORTANT FOR THE CUSTOMER TO TOUCH THE PRODUCT OR OPEN IT UP PRIOR TO PURCHASE?

In some cases, it may be important that the customer see the product in its entirety or open the package. For example, they may want to try out the clasp or fastener on a purse. If so, the packaging will need to be easily resealable. A clear cellophane reusable bag, a container with a lid, and a box with a cutout all qualify.

DO YOUR PRODUCTS BECOME WRINKLED EASILY?

Many products in this category are prone to wrinkles. Instead of folding, consider rolling the product and using a wrap or a bellyband to package it. You can print your brand identity on the wrap, using techniques such as stamping, block printing, or stenciling, or if you're fulfilling bulk orders, pre-printed wraps or bellybands might be best.

DO YOU NEED TO DIFFERENTIATE BETWEEN SIZES OR STYLES WITHIN A BUDGET?

Hangtags or inserts that feature pre-printed information offer a budget-smart solution for stating various sizes and styles. For instance, all the sizes you make can be pre-printed on the tag, and each individual garment's size can be circled or punched when you attach the tag to the product.

designer spotlight
GENERAL KNOT & CO.

After many years in the fashion industry working for well-known international companies, Andrew Payne decided to strike out on his own doing something unique with vintage fabrics, a long-time obsession of his. This was how General Knot & Co. was born.

Q & A

WHAT KIND OF ITEMS DO YOU CREATE?
We design and produce limited-edition neckties, bow ties, pocket squares, and belts using vintage and dead-stock fabrics. Every piece is numbered, based on the limited quantity being made.

WHERE DO YOU SELL YOUR GOODS?
We have a very popular website, but our largest growth is wholesale, especially in Japan. We also sell wholesale to upmarket menswear boutiques in the US, and have a growing trade in the UK and Europe.

HOW ARE THEY PACKAGED WHEN SOLD?
All our boxes and papers are made from recycled kraft, including the crinkle stuffing inside the boxes. Each tie comes with a manila cutting ticket as a hangtag, on which we hand-stamp the style number and its limited-edition number. We wrap each box with cotton twill tape, securing it with a kraft logo sticker.

WHY DID YOU DECIDE TO PACKAGE THEM IN THIS WAY?
Packaging is an essential part of your marketing and tells your customer the level of care you are putting into each step of the process, both visually and in terms of shipping considerations.

DID YOU CONSIDER USING OTHER PACKAGING MATERIALS?
We always knew we wanted kraft because it's consistent with our brand's simple sophistication. We do play around with different box shapes and different tape colors, and we are always looking to finesse the presentation.

WHAT DO YOU THINK MAKES FOR IMPACTFUL PACKAGING WHEN SELLING TO A CUSTOMER?
To keep the product neat on a table presentation we opted for a kraft bellyband with a slit for the cutting tag, keeping the tie held neatly but with the limited-edition feature still prominent.

ARE THERE ANY ECO-FRIENDLY ELEMENTS TO YOUR PACKAGING?
Our packaging, hangtags, and packing materials are all recycled and recyclable.

WHAT SPECIAL CONSIDERATIONS ARE THERE FOR SHIPPING YOUR GOODS?
The protective crinkle kraft paper we nest our products in ensures they arrive in ready-to-wear condition. We are also lucky that our product is pliable, so there is no risk of damage in normal shipping situations.

Opposite: Kraft paper boxes with tissue paper and crinkle paper padding.
This page left: Hand-stamped manila ticket hangtags.
This page right: Printed kraft label.

designer spotlight
FOG LINEN WORK

Initially an importer of used books and housewares, Yumiko Sekine saw a gap in the marketplace for daily-use linen products. Her first collection consisted of just seven items. Today, Fog Linen Work produces a large line of linen fashion and home products. Yumiko's brand and packaging reflect her desire to create beautiful, simple products.

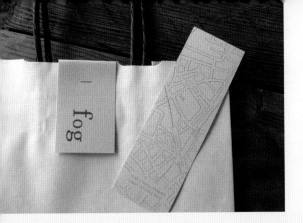

Q & A

WHAT KIND OF ITEMS DO YOU CREATE?
Fog Linen Work designs and creates products for everyday life, including adult and baby clothing, kitchen linens, and home products.

WHERE DO YOU SELL YOUR GOODS?
We are based in Tokyo, Japan and sell to stores around the world.

HOW ARE THEY PACKAGED WHEN SOLD?
I chose cotton muslin bags to package our baby clothing. Each is hand-stamped with a line drawing of the item, product information, and our website URL. Our adult clothing is simply packaged with our company hangtag attached by a linen thread. The packaging of our cloths and aprons is minimal because the product name and specifications are imprinted on the products themselves. Each item is tied with cotton thread, showcasing the description simply but elegantly.

WHY DID YOU DECIDE TO PACKAGE THEM IN THIS WAY?
Our philosophy is about simplicity and advocating a natural lifestyle, so I wanted the packaging to reflect that with plenty of white space in the hangtag design. For the baby clothing, I wanted the packaging to have a touch of cuteness to it.

DID YOU CONSIDER USING OTHER PACKAGING MATERIALS?
I considered using clear bags for the baby clothing to showcase the products without having to open the packaging. Ultimately, I felt that option was not as charming as the cotton bag. I decided to stamp the product outlines onto the cotton bag again so people could see the contents without having to open the package.

WHAT DO YOU THINK MAKES FOR IMPACTFUL PACKAGING WHEN SELLING TO A CUSTOMER?
I think packaging should be simple and informative.

ARE THERE ANY ECO-FRIENDLY ELEMENTS TO YOUR PACKAGING?
I was striving to minimize the amount of material used and was careful to choose materials that the customer could possibly reuse.

WHAT SPECIAL CONSIDERATIONS ARE THERE FOR SHIPPING YOUR GOODS?
I like to package my products compactly and ensure they are well cushioned to avoid possible damage during transportation.

Opposite: Stamped fabric bag and paper tags.
This page left: Stamped paper tags and paper bag.
This page right: Printed fabric mitten bag.

DESIGNING YOUR PACKAGING

SOFT FURNISHINGS

This is a category where the patterns and details on a product may play an important role in its overall packaging. Customers tend to purchase tea towels, napkins, and cushions because they are drawn to the design or motif, so including such elements in the packaging is a good strategy to reinforce your brand. As these products are generally textile-based, customers often like to feel them before purchasing. Whether you sell the products in sets or as single units, this will influence your packaging, as will the need to protect them from getting dirty or wet. Some of the items discussed in this chapter are cushions and pillows, napkins, towels, blankets, and throws.

This page: Cushion in kimono-style, hand-printed wrapping by Nicole James, Yardage Design.
Opposite: Hand-printed, rolled napkins by Viola E. Sutanto, Chewing the Cud.

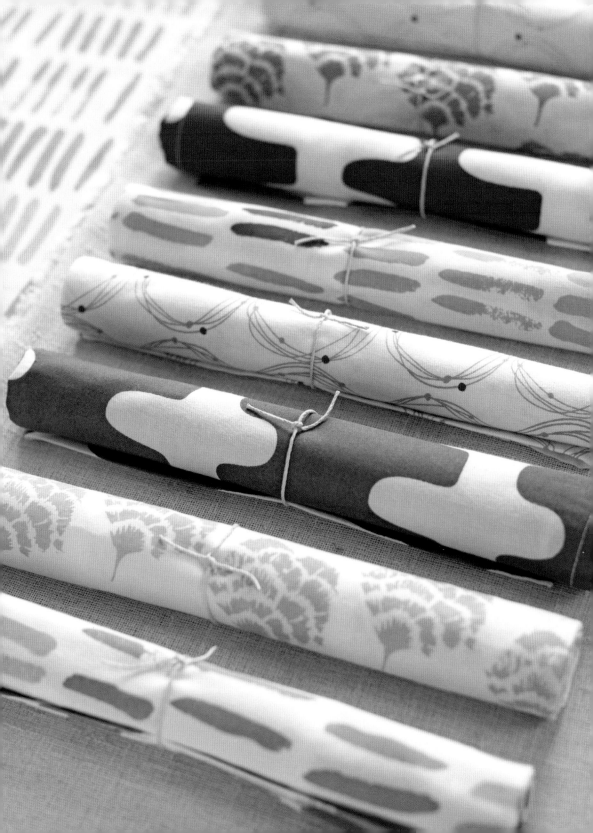

PACKAGING MATTERS

This is another category where the tactile and visual can play a vital role in securing a sale. Often, customers are buying into more than just the functionality of the product; they are lured by the aesthetic and style. Yet minimizing potential damage is equally important when creating its packaging. Here we delve into some of these issues.

IS IT IMPORTANT THAT THE CUSTOMER SEES THE PATTERNS OR DESIGNS ON THE PRODUCTS?

Products in this category tend to be design-driven, meaning the patterns and details are big selling points. One way of showcasing them is in containers with a window so that part of the detail is clearly visible. Or you might opt for a transparent material, such as a clear plastic or vellum box, or a glass container. If using opaque packaging, consider printing the product graphics on the outside of the package.

WILL YOUR PRODUCT BE SOLD IN SETS?

If you sell directly to the customer, you have full control of the process. But if you sell through stores, you may have to relinquish some of that control. Products intended as sets may be split and sold individually. In this case, you might want to brand your product at the single-unit level so that each piece has your brand identity. You might also choose to mark your products as "not for individual sale" to discourage retailers from splitting sets.

Fair Trade
Organic 200
Count Cotton

What's *Under* Your Pillow?

Embroidered Book Pillowcase
with a secret design underneath the pillow by Emily Mackey
Approx Size: 50 x 75cm / Made in Britain

IS IT IMPORTANT FOR THE CUSTOMER TO BE ABLE TO FEEL THE PRODUCT?

If you think it is it is important for the customer to be able to touch the product, a wrap or band might be the solution. A full wrap covers almost the entire length of the product, and protects it from dirt and stains, but the customer can still feel the product. For more visibility and to reduce costs, you might consider using skinnier wraps or holding the product together with ties and ribbons.

WHAT IF YOU WANT YOUR CUSTOMERS TO SEE THE COLORS AND STYLES WITHOUT BEING ABLE TO OPEN THE PACKAGE?

In this case, you might consider exposing part of your product by using a transparent material like plastic, cellophane, or glass, but keeping it sealed to discourage customers from opening the container.

Opposite: Tea towel with pre-printed, recycled tag and bound with braid by Leonie Cheung, Papercookie.
This page: Pillowcase with recycled card stock and cellophane sleeve packaging by Emily Mackey, Maxemilia.

WHAT INFORMATION NEEDS TO BE PRESENT ON THE PACKAGING?

Since many products in this category come with care instructions, you'll have to figure out a good way to incorporate them into the packaging. You may choose to put this information on a separate tag, or sew it onto the product itself. If you choose to enclose your product in a sealed package, you may want to put this information on the outside packaging. That way, your customers can view the instructions in-store without having to tamper with the package and potentially damage it. But you'll probably want to affix that same information to the product (however repetitive) because tags, labels, and boxes eventually get lost or thrown away. In many instances, you're legally required to list what your product is made of and its country of origin. Be sure to do your research so your package is compliant.

TIP

Customers purchasing items of this kind are often buying not only the product itself, but also the lifestyle that it represents, so striking, beautifully styled photos of the products in use can be a compelling influence to buy.

DO YOUR PRODUCTS GET EASILY WRINKLED?

Friction causes wrinkling. If your product wrinkles easily, consider packaging it with plastic, because plastic reduces friction. Layering each piece with tissue paper or including inexpensive mesh bags also helps, plus it protects the product from dirt. All of these packaging options can easily be embellished with hand-printing techniques or finishing touches, such as labels, tags, or ribbons.

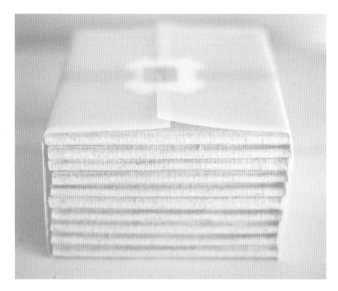

ARE YOUR PRODUCTS LARGE OR BULKY?

To keep overall shipping costs low, lightweight packaging material, such as paper, light fabric, and plastic, is obviously preferable. If you package or ship in a box or container, be sure it is as close to the size of the product as possible, while leaving just enough room for padding. Lightweight bags are also a good option and are quite easy to embellish using block-printing or stenciling techniques (see pages 46-47 and 66-67).

Opposite: Hand-printed napkin with care label by Viola Sutanto, Chewing The Cud.
This page top: Plastic sleeve by Ashley Upchurch, peachlinen.com.
This page bottom: Lasercut tag and pre-printed product sticker by Heather Moore, Skinny laMinx.

designer spotlight
SKINNY LAMINX

Heather Moore is a self-taught illustrator and designer from Cape Town, South Africa. Her label, Skinny laMinx, designs and produces screen-printed fabrics for furnishing and home-sewing. She also creates products like cushions, bags, table runners, and tea towels from her designed fabrics.

Q & A

WHAT KIND OF ITEMS DO YOU CREATE?
All kinds of homewares and stationery products.

WHERE DO YOU SELL YOUR GOODS?
In the Skinny laMinx store in Cape Town, South Africa, in other stores worldwide, and online at skinnylaminx.etsy.com.

HOW ARE THEY PACKAGED WHEN SOLD?
I have hangtags made from patternmaker's card litho-printed with my logo and company details. These are tied around fabric products with jute twine. For paper products, I use round stickers litho-printed in red and black with the brand logo. I wrap items in folded tissue paper, securing them with a branded sticker, tie it up with twine and a lasercut Skinny laMinx bird, upon which I write a little note.

WHY DID YOU DECIDE TO PACKAGE THEM IN THIS WAY?
My designs are simple and clean, so I chose materials that have a simplicity and honesty about them, like patternmakers card, tissue paper, and twine. Also, these are very affordable—an important consideration when starting out.

DID YOU CONSIDER USING OTHER PACKAGING MATERIALS?
This is pretty much the way my packaging has been from the start. At first, my labels were photocopied and now they're litho-printed, as that's more economical now that I produce more.

WHAT DO YOU THINK MAKES FOR IMPACTFUL PACKAGING PRESENTATION WHEN SELLING TO A CUSTOMER?
The most important thing, I think, is to give the impression that you have taken time and care with their package, and that you're giving them something extra along with their purchase.

ARE THERE ANY ECO-FRIENDLY ELEMENTS TO YOUR PACKAGING?
I don't use plastic except on my stationery goods, which need some damage protection. And the cardboard tags, envelopes, and birds are recyclable.

WHAT SPECIAL CONSIDERATIONS ARE THERE FOR SHIPPING YOUR GOODS?
Weight is an important consideration, as I ship abroad a lot, and I try to keep my shipping costs down. When shipping stationery, everything fits a specially designed card envelope, which is both attractive to open and quite sturdy.

Opposite: Tea towels with litho-printed tags tied with twine.
This page left: Die-cut card sleeve.
This page right: Tea towel with litho-printed tag.

designer spotlight
PAPAVER VERT

With her background in store merchandising and fashion design, Patty Benson always had a love for textiles, but it wasn't until a friend taught her how to crochet that she began to explore felting. From this, her bowl designs started to take shape and Papaver Vert was born.

Q & A

WHAT KIND OF ITEMS DO YOU CREATE?
I create handmade felted wool housewares and jewelry.

WHERE DO YOU SELL YOUR GOODS?
Online through my Etsy shop, bricks-and-mortar stores, wholesale, and craft fairs.

HOW ARE THEY PACKAGED WHEN SOLD?
All designs feature woven labels with my business name or logo on them. Items sold in stores also have a hangtag with ticked boxes on the back indicating the felting technique and type of wool. Online or craft fair items (and gift purchases) are packaged in simple, logo-stamped kraft paper boxes, with the product wrapped in white tissue paper, tied with string, and my hangtag attached.

WHY DID YOU DECIDE TO PACKAGE THEM IN THIS WAY?
My nesting bowl sets are specialty pieces and my most popular item, so I wanted them to be "housed" in something when not in use. Having their own special box makes them more valuable.

DID YOU CONSIDER USING OTHER PACKAGING MATERIALS?
I did. A lot! Packaging materials can make or break a product. For me, great packaging always turns heads, regardless of what's being sold.

WHAT DO YOU THINK MAKES FOR IMPACTFUL PACKAGING WHEN SELLING TO A CUSTOMER?
Cohesion. I like to see the company's logo or theme spread across the packaging, labels, or booth displays. Having a distinct identity makes for a powerful statement.

ARE THERE ANY ECO-FRIENDLY ELEMENTS TO YOUR PACKAGING?
My hangtags are printed on recycled paper using soy- and vegetable-based ink from a local printer. My labels are also produced locally.

WHAT SPECIAL CONSIDERATIONS ARE THERE FOR SHIPPING YOUR GOODS?
There are few damage concerns with felt, but I always use plastic bags inside to protect against moisture. I also use tissue paper to help keep the shape of the item.

Opposite: Coaster set with hangtag.
This page left: Coaster set with hangtag.
This page center: Tied coaster set.
This page right: Papier mâché box with hand-stamped detail.

DESIGNING YOUR PACKAGING

PAPER GOODS

In creating an impactful presentation for your paper products, keep in mind that you are essentially selling your artwork, so the customer should be able to easily view it. Whether you sell your products individually or in sets might also drive your packaging decisions. Since paper goods are usually sold at higher quantities and lower price points than other product categories, you'll probably want a cost-efficient, minimal-labor packaging option. Paper products tend to wrinkle and crease easily, so your packaging should also take into account the need for protection against damage, dirt, and humidity. And finally, be sure to use acid-free materials to protect your archival prints.

cooking...

This page: Cooking notebook in cello sleeve by Verónica de Arriba, Depeapa.
Opposite: Stamped geometric gift and party favor bags by Brittni Mehlhoff, Paper & Stitch.

PACKAGING MATTERS

In many ways, the material steers the packaging decisions in this category. After all, you don't really need expensive wooden or ceramic boxes to house your paper goods. Otherwise, the packaging would probably cost more than the product! Let's take a closer look at possible packaging options and concerns for paper items.

ARE YOU SELLING SINGLE ITEMS OR SETS?

If you are selling greeting cards as single units, your price points are likely not high enough to warrant expensive packaging. A clear cellophane sleeve is probably the most cost-effective way of packaging it. Make sure your card is branded (printed on the back or on an insert). However, if you are selling one-of-a-kind books and posters, you might consider investing in a sturdier envelope, bag, or box, all of which can be pre-printed or embellished with blocks, stamps, stencils, or other hand-printing tools.

This page: Letterpress-printed tags and wraps by Alischa Herrmann, Bespoke Letterpress.
Opposite: Twine shipping tags by TJ Hess, Ink & Iron.

IF YOU ARE SELLING DIFFERENT ARTWORK IN SETS, IS IT IMPORTANT FOR THE CUSTOMER TO SEE THE VARIATIONS?

In this category, it's really important that the customer is able to see the artwork before they purchase, so if you are selling in sets, you might want to package them in a box where you can feature the different styles on an adhesive label or a hangtag. That way, the customer will not need to open the packaging, which will hopefully prevent the contents from getting dirty or damaged. On the other hand, if you are selling zines or books, you may actually want the customer to be able to leaf through them before purchase, so your packaging might be resealable. Hand-embellished wraps and bands are also viable options for keeping these bundled products together.

IS TEXTURE A MAJOR SELLING FACTOR FOR YOUR PRODUCT?

For letterpress, embossed, or stamp-foiled cards and prints, consider using
a clear or thin packaging so customers can feel the texture, or at least view it
clearly. After all, the specialty printing is what warrants the premium pricing,
so be proud to show it off.

This page: Letterpress-printed tags and wraps by Alischa Herrmann,
Bespoke Letterpress.
Opposite top: Stationery set in kraft card box with branded band and hangtag
by Suzanne Hayley, Paper Ivy.
Opposite bottom: Luggage tag calendar, laser-printed on recycled paper by
Stacie Humpherys, Girl*In*Gear Studio.

HOW DO SIZE AND WEIGHT IMPACT YOUR PACKAGING?

While prints and cards are lightweight, books can be quite heavy, which of course means increased packaging and shipping costs. If your sales are mostly online and you are generally selling single units, a simple bubble-lined or cardboard mailer with your brand on it could work well. However, if you are fulfilling larger orders, don't be tempted to skimp on your outer packaging. Heavier items require sturdy packaging and reliable sealing. If you are selling oversized posters, consider using a cardboard tube and playing with stencils, stamps, or branded tape and labels.

HOW CAN I PREVENT FOLDS, WRINKLES, AND DAMAGE?

Paper products are often lightweight and easily susceptible to accidental folds and wrinkles. A zine with dog-eared edges, for example, is no longer in pristine condition, and therefore not as appealing. It is a good idea to first wrap a paper product with acid-free tissue paper before you package it. Furthermore, sandwiching a zine or print between two heavier pieces of cardboard not only protects it against wrinkles and unwanted folds, it also prevents dirt and stains from getting onto it. But don't settle for a generic cardboard; this is where you can get really creative! Stencils, rubber stamps, hand-drawn illustrations, paints, and die-cuts are all fair game! Or, seal the cardboard "sandwich" with a branded adhesive label.

designer spotlight
STUDIO CARTA

From her mother, Angela Liguori inherited a love of the tactile, an eye for beauty, and an attention to the details of skilled craftsmanship. After receiving a gift of exquisite stationery, her particular love of beautiful paper and paper objects was born. Having gained valuable experience at various bookmaking and letterpress studios, she interwove her passion for paper and design with her own unique vision to found Studio Carta.

Q & A

WHAT KIND OF ITEMS DO YOU CREATE?
Letterpress cards and stationery, sets of vintage
stamps, and glassine.

WHERE DO YOU SELL YOUR GOODS?
Mostly wholesale and via our online shop.

HOW ARE THEY PACKAGED WHEN SOLD?
Our sets of letterpress cards, vintage stamps, and
glassine are all packaged in differently sized glassine
envelopes. I designed the labels and, in some cases,
I used a custom-made calligraphy label by artist and
illustrator Susy Pilgrim Waters. We print all of our
labels on our studio's laser printer, using circle label
paper produced by the eco-friendly company Waste
Not Paper.

**WHY DID YOU DECIDE TO PACKAGE THEM
IN THIS WAY?**
I prefer to protect our products with eco-friendly
packaging and try to avoid the use of plastic
whenever possible.

**WHAT DO YOU THINK MAKES FOR IMPACTFUL
PACKAGING WHEN SELLING TO A CUSTOMER?**
I believe packaging is one of the key elements in
selling a product. I believe in simple and clean,
yet modern and effective design.

**ARE THERE ANY ECO-FRIENDLY ELEMENTS
TO YOUR PACKAGING?**
Yes, I always prefer to use paper instead of plastic
boxes or bags, and I keep the packaging as simple as
possible, avoiding too much waste.

**WHAT SPECIAL CONSIDERATIONS ARE THERE
FOR SHIPPING YOUR GOODS?**
For shipping our products, again, we use only
recycled paper and cardboard boxes. We prefer not
to use any bubble-wrapping, and we recycle and
reuse any other packaging materials we receive at
our studio.

Opposite: Printed cards for tape measures tied with
cotton ribbon.
This page: Glassine envelopes with laser-printed labels.
Calligraphy on labels by Susy Pilgrim Waters.

designer spotlight
PAPER IVY

Sydney-based designer Suzanne Hayley runs Paper Ivy, a small paper and giftware brand that takes inspiration from natural shapes and geometric order in traditional and modern design and then applies it through a filter of graphic sensibility.

Q & A

WHAT KIND OF ITEMS DO YOU CREATE?
Paper Ivy has evolved from a greeting card design company to one that encompasses a range of stationery, calendars, jewelry, and accessories.

WHERE DO YOU SELL YOUR GOODS?
I sell on Etsy, at art/design and craft markets, and in small boutique stores.

HOW ARE THEY PACKAGED WHEN SOLD?
All Paper Ivy goods have some variation of a belly-band displaying the logo and web address. I then use cellophane sleeves to protect them. The stationery sets come in a black box with a natural kraft lid detailing the contents and design motif.

WHY DID YOU DECIDE TO PACKAGE THEM IN THIS WAY?
Initially, I just wanted something that I thought looked good! However, I wanted minimal, easy-to-make packaging showing the brand but letting the goods speak for themselves.

DID YOU CONSIDER USING OTHER PACKAGING MATERIALS?
I looked at using cardboard envelopes but, for the quantities I produce, it would be more expensive. The other issue was visibility—the customer can't see the product in cardboard.

WHAT DO YOU THINK MAKES FOR IMPACTFUL PACKAGING PRESENTATION WHEN SELLING TO A CUSTOMER?
Create a recognizable brand, one that distinguishes you from everyone else but that's also friendly and approachable. People like to feel a connection. This brand needs to be on all your packaging, products, and communication.

ARE THERE ANY ECO-FRIENDLY ELEMENTS TO YOUR PACKAGING?
The paper bands are 100 percent recycled, as are the boxes used in the stationery sets. The twine is made from jute or cotton.

WHAT SPECIAL CONSIDERATIONS ARE THERE FOR SHIPPING YOUR GOODS?
At markets, I use brown paper lunch bags that I print at home with the Paper Ivy branding. Paper goods usually need a little protection when shipping. The cellophane sleeves help protect from moisture, and anything bigger than a single card is shipped in a rigid mailer. Boxed stationery sets are sent in bubble mailers to protect edges and corners.

Opposite: Stationery box set packaged with a bellyband inside a cardboard box with a printed label.
This page left: Tissue paper wrapping with twine and a printed tag.
This page right: Card set packaged with a bellyband and cellophane wrapping.

DESIGNING YOUR PACKAGING

HOME AND LIVING

Artwork and oversized items obviously tend to be unwieldy, so you'll need to take specific precautions to protect them. Consider both inner, or protective, and outer packaging (both of which can be embellished to reinforce your brand). Due to the sheer size of these packages, delicate embellishments, such as thin ribbons or tiny tags, may get lost. Think in terms of bolder gestures, like your logo on the shipping box, branded packing tape, or a large, striking graphic stenciled on the outer package.

Since oversized items, such as art, furniture, and rugs, are often expensive, it is worth investing in beautiful and functional packaging that helps create a memorable brand experience for the customer.

HEIRLOOM SEED KIT

EDIBLE FLOWERS

EDIBLE

HEIRLOOM SEED KIT

This page: Edible Flower Heirloom seed kit design by Sarah Rainwater and Sarah Verity, Sarah Rainwater Design.
Opposite: Hemp baskets by Laura Johnson and Alexandra Cooke, Nkuku.

PACKAGING MATTERS

Items in this category pose a unique set of considerations—chiefly how to package bulky items beautifully yet practically. Sometimes, less is more. Keeping it simple might be the best solution, as it adds to the wow-factor of the product itself. Let's get familiar with some of the key packaging issues for these items.

HOW DO YOU GET CREATIVE WITH YOUR OUTER PACKAGING?

You will probably be using cardboard or wooden boxes for your oversized items, or large bags if they do not need to be shipped. Think of them as your blank canvases to print, stencil, stamp, or embellish upon. You may even choose to embroider or paint on your packing bag. Pre-printed adhesive labels can add visual interest to your outer packaging, or you might attach tear-resistant tags adorned with your brand identity. Small tags or delicate embellishments tend to look too dainty or insignificant when paired against large items. This is the time to think bold and have fun with oversized tags, larger graphics, and fun decorations. If your item requires a wooden box or crate, you might consider personalizing it with your brand.

This page: Cardboard box decorated with twine and paper feathers by Anastasia Mikailenko, Anastasia Marie.
Opposite: Protective padding made from wood chips and recycled cardboard by Thibaut Malet.

HOW DO YOU BUILD YOUR INNER PACKAGING TO PROTECT YOUR PRODUCT AGAINST DIRT, MOISTURE, AND DAMAGE?

Protecting your product against damage is key for this category, as it will need to be transported off-site once the sale is made. For furniture and large home décor pieces, the safest solution is foam-in-place. This is a liquid polyurethane material that expands into dense, solid foam around the product and creates a custom-shaped protective mold that is strong, lightweight, and reusable.

When packaging a rug, roll it up tightly (with the graphics on the inside), and secure it with packing tape before encasing it in a cardboard box or thick plastic. I would recommend using Tyvek or plastic tags instead of paper ones, because they are unlikely to get damaged. Tie them using heavy-duty twine or affix plastic ties with a tagging gun. Your tag is a good and easy-to-implement branding opportunity.

In the case of prints and certain types of paintings (e.g., watercolors), use acid-free tissue to cover them, and for additional protection against moisture, wrap them again in plastic. If these are regular products for you, investing in some clear plastic sleeves might be an economical option. Sandwich the wrapped painting between corrugated cardboard sheets.

For larger canvases or framed pieces, you'll also need a sturdier outer container as well as corner edge protectors. Many companies offer specialist boxes and containers for shipping artwork (see Resources, pages 170-71). Once suitably packaged, you can really get creative with the exterior using many of the techniques we've already talked about. Hand-print the cardboard pieces, or tape them with pre-printed shipping tape featuring your company name and logo.

HOW DO YOU BUILD YOUR PACKAGING TO PROTECT YOUR PRODUCT AGAINST DIRT, MOISTURE, AND DAMAGE?

Baskets and containers are usually packaged in boxes, padded with foam all around. If your container has handles, it might be a good idea to first wrap them in bubble wrap to protect against damage. To minimize waste and movement, you'll want to pick a box that is roughly 2 inches (5cm) bigger on all sides than your container.

WHAT INFORMATION NEEDS TO BE PRESENT ON THE OUTER PACKAGING?

If you are shipping your products, it is important to label them accurately. For instance, having "fragile" or "this side up" labels will alert the shipper of the product's fragility, although can't always guarantee special handling. Nevertheless, it is worth the extra effort to try to protect your product.

IS SEALING IMPORTANT?

No matter how beautiful your packaging is, if it is not sealed properly, the product could become damaged. Always use strong packing tape (the heavier the package, the thicker the tape) and reinforce it with an extra layer if necessary. You can also choose to custom-print your tape with your brand.

ARE YOUR ITEMS HIGH-PRICED? WHAT SPECIAL FINISHING TOUCHES CAN YOU ADD TO ENHANCE THE BRAND EXPERIENCE?

For a higher-priced item, consider adding something to the package to enhance both the customer experience and your brand. Perhaps a printed insert or card with a personalized customer message signed by the maker is the ideal finishing touch. If it is a limited-edition piece, you might consider designing a certificate of ownership or authenticity. In the case of baskets or containers, you might choose to fill them with something special as a token of appreciation.

TIPS

For greater impact, why not use some beautiful ribbon and maybe a super-sized hangtag or wax seal for a unique finishing touch!

If you're shipping the product, place some transparent tape over the shipping label to keep it in place during transport.

Opposite: "Handle with care" rubber stamp by Anastasia Mikailenko, Anastasia Marie.
This page: Kraft envelope with personalized sealing tag by Hadrien Monloup, Bellroy.

designer spotlight
Jonah Silver

Jonah Silver is an independent furniture and product designer based in London. Although he initially studyied scenic construction, he came to realize that he would rather create things that were more permanent and lasting. The result is a collection of furniture and housewares based on the idea of longevity; his products can be used for many generations and actually become better with time and use.

Q & A

WHAT KIND OF ITEMS DO YOU CREATE?

I create carefully designed, one-of-a-kind pieces of furniture as well as smaller, handmade wooden items such as cutting boards with a focus on finish and material. I use ecologically friendly woods and reclaimed materials where possible.

WHERE DO YOU SELL YOUR GOODS?

My work is currently available only through my website. Since most of my products are one-of-a-kind pieces, I prefer to work on commission.

HOW ARE THEY PACKAGED WHEN SOLD?

When selling smaller items such as breadboards, I use recycled paper and packaging. I have a large stock of interesting printed paper collected from various countries which I then combine with kraft paper and string.

WHY DID YOU DECIDE TO PACKAGE THEM IN THIS WAY?

This method of packaging reflects the handcrafted and environmentally conscious nature of my products. It also extends my personal brand.

WHAT DO YOU THINK MAKES FOR IMPACTFUL PACKAGING WHEN SELLING TO A CUSTOMER?

Packaging should tell part of a greater story, a story that includes the store, the brand, and the product itself. All of these elements have to work together in order to have a real impact on customers.

ARE THERE ANY ECO-FRIENDLY ELEMENTS TO YOUR PACKAGING?

Most of my product packaging is recycled or reused in some way, and I encourage my customers to continue this process by reusing it themselves.

WHAT SPECIAL CONSIDERATIONS ARE THERE FOR SELLING/SHIPPING YOUR GOODS?

When shipping, I use air packs as protection. They're lightweight, which means the packages are lighter, more economical, and environmentally friendly.

Opposite: Steel, ash, and corduroy sofa.
This page left and right: Breadboard wrapped in cardboard and printed paper with a kraft paper tag.

SUITABILITY OF DIFFERENT PACKAGING MATERIALS

Contents/Material	Cardboard	Glass	Plastic	Wood
Food/ Perishables	♥	♥	♥	♥
Bath/ Beauty products		♥	♥	
Metal, Glass & Ceramic items	♥		♥	♥
Furniture	♥			♥
Clothes, Shoes & Accessories	♥	♥	♥	♥
Artwork, Canvases & Sculpture	♥		♥	♥
Jewelry	♥		♥	♥
Soft Furnishings	♥		♥	
Paper Goods	♥		♥	♥

PAPER WEIGHTS

Listed here are the most common and widely available paper types and weights—with their metric equivalents. Japanese standards are different, so take this into account and follow the manufacturer's guidelines.

Note the differences from one paper type to another. This is because papers bulk differently due to many factors, such as how compact the fibers are, how they are pressed, along with what's in the pulp and the size of the uncut sheet.

Basic weight	Grams per square meter
Bond Stock paper	
13lb	49gsm
16lb	61gsm
20lb	75gsm
24lb	90gsm
28lb	105gsm
32lb	120gsm
36lb	135gsm
40lb	151gsm
Cover Stock paper (also known as Card Stock)	
50lb	135gsm
60lb	163gsm
65lb	176gsm
80lb	216gsm
90lb	243gsm
100lb	271gsm
110lb	298gsm
130lb	352gsm
160lb	433gsm
Newsprint Stock	
22lb	36gsm
28lb	46gsm
30lb	49gsm
32lb	52gsm
34lb	55gsm
35lb	57gsm

GLOSSARY

Acid-free
A paper product having a pH of 7 or above, making it archival.

Appliqué
Applying pieces of one material to another, usually by sewing.

Block Printing
The printing of images or designs using carved wood or lino blocks.

Ceramic Paint
Solvent-based opaque color for crockery, glass, metal, and other non-porous surfaces.

Cold-pressed
A paper with slight surface texture produced by pressing the sheet between cold cylinders.

Decal
A design prepared on special paper for transfer onto another surface, e.g., wood, metal, etc.

Die-Cut
A cutting method that uses a machine to punch out shapes.

Embossing
Creating a raised image on paper.

Faux Finish
A technique that imitates the look of a natural material.

Gilding
Applying a thin metallic foil, such as gold leaf, to a surface.

Glassine
A strong, smooth, transparent, or semi-transparent paper, resistant to air and grease.

Glaze
A transparent layer of varnish or diluted paint.

Grommet (or Eyelet)
A small metal ring for reinforcing holes in paper or fabric.

Inkjet Printer
Computer printers that spray ink onto the paper, as opposed to a laser printer, which fuses powder (toner) onto the paper with heat.

Linocut
An image is drawn or transferred to a linoleum block, which is then cut with small carving tools.

Masking Tape
A low-tack adhesive tape.

Matte or Flat Finish
A surface or coating that is dull or non-glossy.

Metallic Paint
A solvent-based paint able to adhere to metals.

Offset or Lithographic Printing
Images or text on metal plates are transferred to rubber blankets and the print material.

Parchment (or Vellum)
A hard-finished, slightly translucent paper.

Patina (also Verdigris)
A coating, that forms on copper and bronze due to oxidization.

pH Value
Measurement of the acidity or alkalinity in paper.

Polymer Clay
Malleable modeling clay, which is hardened by baking.

Quadrille Paper or Graph Paper
Paper printed with a faint grid.

Rag Paper
Paper made from 50 to 100 percent cotton or linen fiber.

Relief Print
Any print in which the image is printed from the raised area of a carved, etched, or cast block.

Rubbing (or Frottage)
Taking an impression from a raised patterned area by rubbing.

Screen Printing
A printing method where a stencil is adhered to a fine screen, through which ink is squeegeed.

Stippling
A dabbing motion to apply small amounts of paint.

Transfer Medium or Solution
A solvent that reactivates the ink in toner-based photocopies.

Tyvek Fabric
A strong, synthetic material made from spun polythene fibers.

Varnish
A protective coating used over a finished painting or object.

Washi
Wa, meaning "Japanese," and *shi,* meaning "paper"; a tough paper often made from gampi tree fibers.

TEMPLATES

BOXES

These packaging templates are easy to download, resize, and print. You can photocopy them, resizing according to your needs, or simply scan the corresponding QR codes and download.

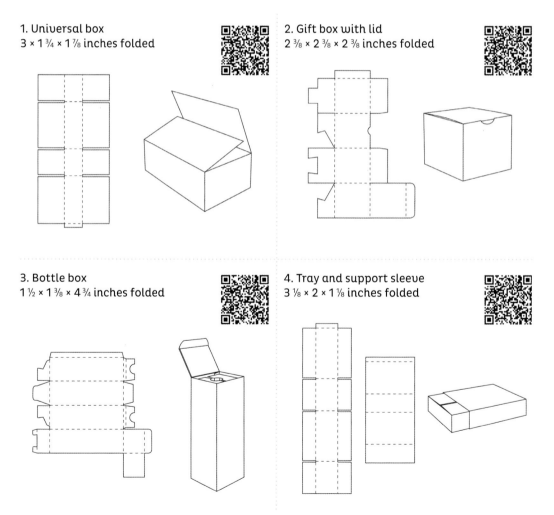

1. Universal box
3 × 1 ¾ × 1 ⅞ inches folded

2. Gift box with lid
2 ⅜ × 2 ⅜ × 2 ⅜ inches folded

3. Bottle box
1 ½ × 1 ⅜ × 4 ¾ inches folded

4. Tray and support sleeve
3 ⅛ × 2 × 1 ⅛ inches folded

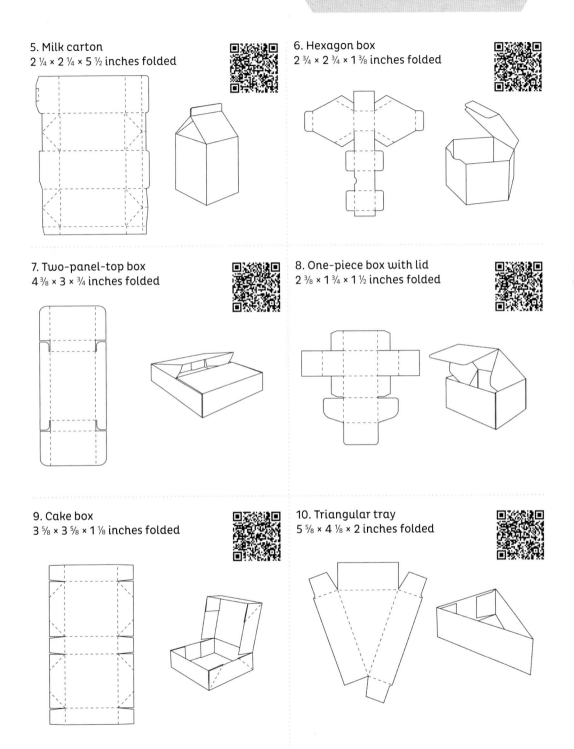

5. Milk carton
2 ¼ × 2 ¼ × 5 ½ inches folded

6. Hexagon box
2 ¾ × 2 ¾ × 1 ⅜ inches folded

7. Two-panel-top box
4 ⅜ × 3 × ¾ inches folded

8. One-piece box with lid
2 ⅜ × 1 ¾ × 1 ½ inches folded

9. Cake box
3 ⅝ × 3 ⅝ × 1 ⅛ inches folded

10. Triangular tray
5 ⅝ × 4 ⅛ × 2 inches folded

167

LABELS

1.

2.

3.

4.

5.

6.

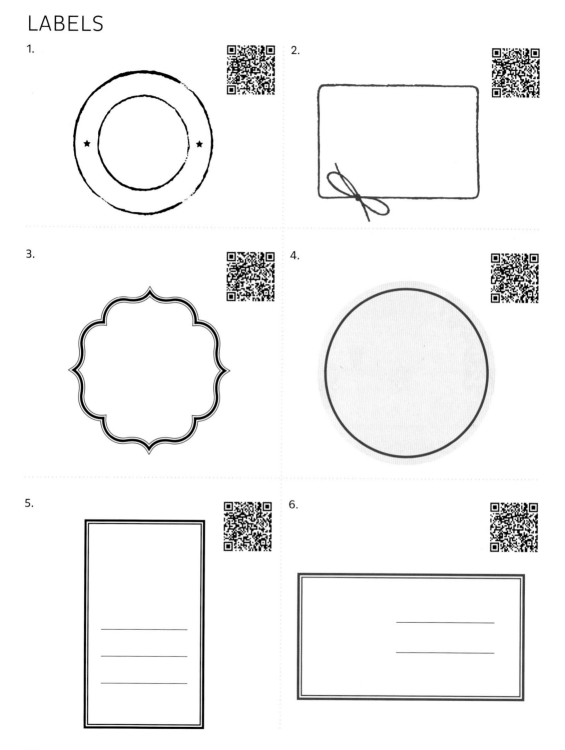

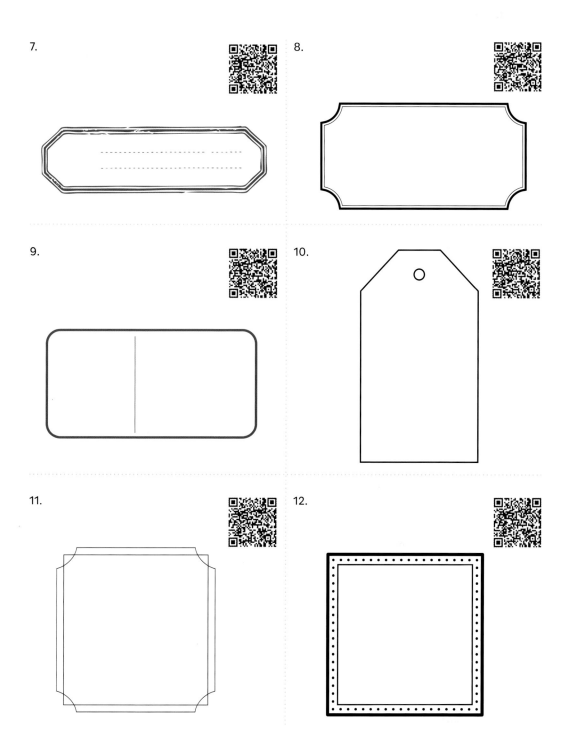

7.

8.

9.

10.

11.

12.

USEFUL INFORMATION

WEBSITES

ceramicartsdaily.org – a wonderful resource for all things ceramic, including forums, tips, and advice

craftster.org – offbeat, online craft community sharing ideas, articles, tips, and news

dawanda.com – online marketplace for buying and selling a range of products

etsy.com – site for crafters and designer-makers to sell their goods

folksy.com – buying and selling site for crafts and gifts

lovelypackage.com – showcases innovative packaging trends across a broad range of products

supermarkethq.com – selling site for designers and designer-makers

thedieline.com – site dedicated to the package design industry

SUPPLIERS

NORTH AMERICA AND CANADA

americancontainers.com – wide range of containers for a variety of products

barenforum.org – woodblock printmaking resource

clearimageprinting.com – offers a range of printing services and finishes

craftoutletusa.com – wholesale craft supply seller

createforless.com – discount craft supplies

dharmatrading.com – fiber art and fabric supplies

frenchpaper.com – large range of paper and envelopes, as well as custom manufacturing services such as embossing

freundcontainer.com – canning jars, as well as other glass and plastic packaging products

greenerprinter.com – digital and offset printers offering fully eco-friendly printing solutions

hankodesigns.com – Asian craft supplies

infinitystamps.com – supplies for DIY metal-stamping

japanesepaperplace.com – variety of Japanese papers

logotags.com – pre-printed metal tags

metprinters.com – Canadian carbon-neutral digital and offset printing services

packaging-usa.com – offer a very wide range of packaging solutions

paper-source.com – a huge variety of paper products and wraps, as well as workshops

papermart.com – enormous selection of bags, boxes, baskets, cards, ribbons, tapes, etc.

thepapermillstore.com – paper and card stock as well as envelopes, labels, etc.

usbox.com – general packaging supplies (boxes, bags, pouches, etc.)

waxseals.com – custom wax seal suppliers

westernspecialty.com – large selection of containers and tins

UK

empirepackaging.co.uk – very broad range of packaging items as well as handy tips and guides

gogreenerbags.co.uk – suppliers of cotton, jute, woven, and non-woven polypropylene bags

macfarlanepackaging.com – boasting 20,000 different packaging materials and products

plutopackaging.co.uk – large cross-section of packaging material and products

ptgdigital.com – digital and offset printing services

rkburt.com – Japanese and handmade papers, also general paper supplies

thejapaneseshop.co.uk – wide selection of Japanese papers and Washi tapes, etc.

tinyboxcompany.co.uk – Don't think there is a box product these guys can't supply! They also stock a range of ribbons, tissue papers, and bags

AUSTRALIA AND NEW ZEALAND
finepapers.com.au/japanese – papers

marketingefficiencies.com.au – digital and offset printing services

origami.com.au

CHINA
globalsources.com – directory of paper manufacturers and suppliers

GERMANY
dahlinger.com – luxury packaging and display products, from boxes and jewelry packaging to elasticated tags and bespoke labels

BOOKS AND MAGAZINES

Handmade Packaging Workshop: Tips, Tools & Techniques for Creating Custom Bags, Boxes and Containers – Rachel Wiles; HOW Books (US); UK edition called **Handmade Packaging Workshop: Tutorials and Professional Advice for Creating Handcrafted Boxes, Labels, Bags and More** - Thames & Hudson (UK), 2012

I Heart Stationery: Inspirational Techniques, Materials, and Practitioners – Charlotte Rivers; Universe Publishing, NY (US); Jacqui Small LLP (UK), 2012

Print Workshop: Hand-Printing Techniques and Truly Original Projects – Christine Schmidt; a Potter Craft publication (imprint of Random House), 2010

Printing by Hand: A Modern Guide to Printing with Handmade Stamps, Stencils, and Silk Screens – Lena Corwin; Stewart, Tabori & Chang (imprint of Harry N. Abrams, Inc.), 2008

Selling Your Crafts Online: With Etsy, eBay, and Pinterest – Michael Miller; Que Publishing, 2013

The Packaging Designer's Book of Patterns – László Roth and George L. Wybenga; John Wiley & Sons, Inc.; 2013

TRADE SHOWS AND FESTIVALS

artfaircalendar.com – USA-wide fine art fair and craft show listings

bazaarbizarre.org - avant-garde craft fairs in Boston, Cleveland, and San Francisco

craftevents.com.au – arts and crafts fairs for Australia and New Zealand

craftscouncil.org.uk – resource for all crafts people based in the UK

www.ithacafestival.org – annual crafts festival, New York State

packagingdesignconference.com - organized by Dieline, this design conference focuses solely on the package design industry and package designers

renegadecraft.com - contemporary craft and design fairs across the US, as well as London, UK

ukcraftfairs.com – UK-wide fine craft show listings

INDEX

CONTRIBUTOR INDEX

1 Trick Pony
1trickpony.com
Photos by Mike Mielcarz

Amanda Guarini
A Guarini Design
aguarinidesign.com
Photos by Mary Beth Manifold

Nikki Mihalik
Akula Kreative
akulakreative.com
Yellow felt DVD pocket
photo by Caroline Tran

Lucía Elizondo
Anagrama
anagrama.com
Photos by Caroga Photographer

Anastasia Mikailenko
Anastasia Marie
anastasiamariecards.com

Beatrice Menis
cargocollective.com/beatrice-menis
Photos by Mara Rodriguez

Hadrien Monloup
Bellroy
bellroy.com

Alischa Herrmann
Bespoke Letterpress
bespokepress.com.au

**Marianne Gardner
and Sean Maginity
Bird and Feather**
birdandfeather.com

Chris MacManus
Bittle & Burley
bittleandburley.com
Photos by Victoria Rich

Danie Pout
BLANK
blankgoods.com.au

Aubrey Levitt
Body & Eden
bodyandeden.com
Design by Jennifer Schwartz
Photoss by Joshua Targownik

BRND WGN
Designers: Glenn Grech,
Roberta Galea, Kris Vella Petroni
brndwgn.com
Photos by Glenn Grech, Karl Attard

Nicole Ebbitt
The Caramel Jar
thecarameljar.com
Photos by The Caramel Jar and
Jonathan Young

Kat Miller
Cardinal House
cardinal-house.com

Viola E. Sutanto
Chewing the Cud
chewingthecud.com
Photos by Kristen Loken

Janet Coffman
Circle 21 Candles
www.circle21candles.com
Design by Studio Nudge
Photos by Andrew Cebulka

Yoko Tamaki
Come Comer
yoook823.wix.com
Label design by Kumi
Kagawa Matsumoto

Beatriz Gaspar
Con Botas de Agua
conbotasdeagua.com

Ashley Connelly
The Creative Place
thecreativeplace.blogspot.com

Foant Asour & Aliki Rovithi
DEDE DextrousDesign
dede.gr

Verónica de Arriba
Depeapa
depeapa.com
Photos by Argider Aparicio

Divine Dairy
divinedairy.com.au
Design by Frank Aloi Design Co
– frankaloi.com.au

**Elizabeth Pawle – Elizabeth
Pawle Illustration**
elizabethpawle.etsy.com
Photos by Francis Pawle

Kirsten Elyse Nurge
Elysium Apothecary
ElysiumApothecary.etsy.com

Amber Corcoran
Fancy Tiger Crafts
fancytigercrafts.com
Design by Fancy Tiger Crafts,
Jaime Jennings, Dan Meyers,
Turnip Design by Heidi Murray

Yumiko Sekine
Fog Linen Work
foglinenwork.com
Photos by Marisa Shimamoto

Andrew Payne
General Knot & Co.
Generalknot.com
Photos by Melisa Cardona

Stacie Humpherys
Girl *In* Gear Studio
girlingearstudio.com
Photos by Stacie Humpherys,
Heidi Adnum

Hovard Design
hovarddesign.com
Photos by Andy Babb, Matt Young,
Michael Gross

TJ Hess
Ink & Iron
inkandiron.com
Photos by Calynn Berry

Gemma Behrens
Jac Whippet
JacWhippet.etsy.com

Jonah Silver
www.jonahsilver.com

Frederick Bouchardy
Joya
joyastudio.com
Photos by Alick Crossley, Bon
Duke, Atif Ateeq

Amber, Heather & Alyssa
Overton Joyful Creations
joyfulcreationsart.etsy.com

Karola Torkos
Karola Torkos Jewellery
karakola.com

Alessandra Taccia – Knots
lacasita-alessandrataccia.blog
spot.co.uk

Dominique Gros
L'art de la Curiosite
lartdelacuriosite.blogspot.com

Kyoko Bowskill
LINK
thelinkcollective.com
Photos by Martin Holtkamp

Jen O'Connor
The Little
Ragamuffin
thelittleragamuffin.com

Grazina Thompson
Lushleys Ltd
Lushleys.co.uk
Packaging by Meridian
(Specialty Packaging) Ltd
Label design by Dovile
Klepaciute, Lushleys Ltd

Emily Mackey
Maxemilia
maxemilia.com
Package design by Ben Cox

Meghann Rader
www.meghannrader.com

Amie Nilsson
Merino Kids
www.merinokids.com

Rachel Ball
Mignon Kitchen Co.
mignonkitchenco.com

Judith Parker
Mine Design
minedesignhome.com
Photos by Laura Plansker

Michaela Houston
Mondän
JewelrybyMondaen.etsy.com

Jessica Wilcox
Modern Moments Designs
modernmomentsdesigns.com

Jamie Jones
Mrs. Jones' Soapbox
mrsjonessoapbox.com

Laura Johnson and
Alexandra Cooke
Nkuku
nkuku.com
Photos by Phil Conrad,
Alice Carfrae

Rachel Mueller
Oil & Wax
oilandwax.com

Grace Kang
Olive Box
myolivebox.com
Photos by Alice Gao

Natalie Jost
Olive Manna
olivemanna.com

Liz Cook
One Seed
oneseedcompany.com
Photos by Liz Cook, Peter Tarasiuk

Nicole Dunphy
Pandora Bell
pandorabell.ie
Design by Rebecca Barker,
Studio Output
Photos by Ken Coleman

Patty Benson
Papaver Vert
www.papaververt.com
Label design by Jillian Clark

Katerina Sachova
Papelote
papelote.cz
Photos by Filip Sach

Brittni Mehlhoff
Paper & Stitch
papernstitchblog.com

Suzanne Hayley
Paper Ivy
www.paperivy.com

Leonie Cheung
Papercookie
papercookie.com.au

Jenny Montgomery
Paper Sushi
papersushishop.com

Piebox
piebox.com
Photos by Steven Karl Metzer
Photography Ltd

Janell Anderson
Prunella Soap
www.cooljanedesign.com

Rae Dunn
www.raedunn.com

Rewined Candles
rewinedcandles.com
Design by Stitch Design Co
Photos by Beau Burdette

Sarah Meredith
Rock Cakes
rockcakes.com

Sarah Rainwater Design
srainwater.com
Design by Sarah Rainwater,
Sarah Verity, Elaine Dunlap

Heather Moore
Skinny LaMinx
Skinnylaminx.com

Angela Liguori
Studio Carta
angelaliguori.com

Swear Words designs:
Loving Earth Luvju tea brand
packaging p.8
Photo by Sean Fennessey –
seanfennessy.com.au
The Butter Factory dairy
labels p.45
McIvor Estate wine
packaging p.98
Springhill Pantry p.109
Photo by Estelle Judah –
estellejudah.com.au

Amy Kelly
That Winsome Girl
thatwinsomegirl.com

Thibaut Malet
www.thibautmalet.com

Jude Winnall
VanillaKiln
VanillaKiln.co.uk

Furze Chan
With Her Animal Poetry
furzechan.com

Nicole James
Yardage Design
yardagedesign.com.au